Visions of a Sacred Truth

AN AKASHIC JOURNEY

L.B. Owens

BALBOA.
PRESS
A DIVISION OF HAY HOUSE

Cover Design front and back created by Ericka Estrella and Sheldon Chick

ISBN: 978-1-4525-6182-0 (sc)
ISBN: 978-1-4525-6183-7 (e)
ISBN: 978-1-4525-6184-4 (hc)

Library of Congress Control Number: 2012920015

Balboa Press books may be ordered through booksellers or by contacting:

Balboa Press
A Division of Hay House
1663 Liberty Drive
Bloomington, IN 47403
www.balboapress.com
1-(877) 407-4847

Printed in the United States of America

Balboa Press rev. date: 11/29/2012

Dedication

For Mom and Dad, Ben, Candy, both of my grandparents
and to everyone else on this planet

Acknowledgements

THIS BOOK WOULD NOT have been possible without the encouragement and support of my family. To my sons John and Nathan, thank you for your love, understanding and the laughter that you bring into my life every day. To my daughter-in-law Sheila, thank you for all your love, support and the light you bring to this family. To my little munchkin Kalvin, who helps me see the world with fresh new loving eyes. Who has also, taught me to always keep asking Why.

I give thanks to the Great Creator, Goddess Divine, divine intervention, my Ancestors and my loving Guides for helping me to keep true to who I am and gently guiding me down the path to enlightenment.

Thanks goes to my sisters for the late night memories and the laughter they bring to my life. Thanks goes to Haley, Charlie and Josh for their loving support. To all my nieces and nephews thank you. Thanks also goes to Mike for all your support. To Bob and his support. To my parents and grandparents I give special gratitude for being a special part of my life. We will meet again.

To Samantha Bichon, I thank you for being my teacher, confidant and loving friend. Bless you for your endless support and encouragement. Thank you Wally for your friendship and support also.

I give thanks to Krista for introducing me to my first past life regression and for your loving friendship.

Many thanks goes to the wonder twins Ericka Estella and Sheldon Chick. Their artistic eye and creative minds created a beautiful work of art-the cover of this book. Ericka is also the model on the cover of the book. Thank you both with all my heart for the work you have done and taking my breath away whenever, I see the cover that so moves me.

I want to thank my publishing company and all the hard work they do.

I would like to thank my students for their support, hard work and encouraging words when I need it the most. I'm proud of all of you. Tiffany, Liz, Mary, Tia, Alex, Shannon, Mimi, Michelle, Tina, Nikki, Phill, Brian, Michael, Amanda, Jennifer, Patricia, Jeanne, Jessica, Lakisha, Brenna, Bryson, and Bailee.

To everyone else that has walked into my life even though it was a short time or even a long period of time. I thank you for the experience and friendship. To the rest of my friends and family and to everyone else who's name was not in the acknowledgements for lack of space. I have not forgotten you. Thank you all for stepping on to my path and walking along for awhile with me.

Foreword

$\mathfrak{T}$HE MAKING OF THIS book has been a long and spiritual journey. The visions/dreams that I have experienced have made me fully aware that the people, places and events that I write about actually existed at certain times in history. My historical research has taken me to the countries and cities that I have dreamed about - places that I didn't know existed in this lifetime. Throughout my travels, I saw time and time again the buildings, mountains and villages of my dreams. This book is based on historical fact, my own personal experiences, and my research and travel.

For instance: Montségur, France was a Cathar stronghold until the Catholic Pope Innocent III mobilized the French army in an attempt to eliminate the heretics, causing the horrendous death by burning of approximately 224 men, women and children. Puivert and Carcassonne, France were also known to the Cathars, as the rulers of those two cities were tolerant of the Cathar religion and both were safe havens for them. Both Puivert and Carcassonne were prominent in my dreams/visions as I detail in this book.

Historical facts show that the Albigensian Crusade, a 45 year military campaign initiated by the Catholic Church to eliminate Catharism, started in 1209 and lasted through 1255 in Languedoc.

Trier, Germany was also the site of a great war against witchcraft from 1581 through 1593. This persecution extended to the Jewish and Protestant people of that region. Trier has the distinction of being the location of one of the biggest mass execution sites in Europe; 368 men, women, children (and even black cats) were killed there.

I am not advocating nor do I condone hatred or intolerance of any religion, Cathar, Catholic, Protestant and the list could go on. One of my reasons for writing this book is to bring into focus the fact that we are all immortal, spiritual beings. Basically, we are all spirit living in a material world. We co-exist in this ever changing world. The path we choose, whether good or bad, is our life lesson to learn. Our life is our chance to make a change for the better. To learn and to realize once and for all that we are all connected to each other and to the Creator. Everything that happens comes from divine purpose. As we live side by side in this theater of life, we have the opportunity to grow as spiritual beings toward enlightenment.

This has been my journey and path. All of the characters mentioned in the book are people and friends that have walked this journey with me. I have taken some creative license and changed certain identifying information to protect the personal privacy of others.

All historical facts regarding The Albigensian Crusade or Cathar Crusade and the Trier Witch Trials are easily accessible on the Internet or at the Library

Prologue

The Dream

My dress is rustling against the cobblestone road. The cool breeze touches my skin like a kiss in spring. I wear a heavy satin dress. Diamonds and other jewels have been sewn on with golden thread. Sea blue is the color of the dress. It suits me. The bodice I wear is quilted and has been tied in the back. I have a servant, which means I have status.

My breathing is heavy and labored in anticipation of what will soon come.

My emotions are mixed; I feel happy, worried and anxious at the same time. I walk slowly toward a building. I can feel someone behind me. I turn to see a tall, thin, flinty-eyed man standing behind me. I know he is my regent and also a cousin. I know he is the conservator of my late father's estate. I am a wealthy woman or should I say a wealthy young woman. I must be only fifteen, though I'm much wiser than my years.

As I turn to look up at the building before me, I see wooden stairs that are heavy and old ascending quite high to the door on the second floor. The stairs are on the exterior of the building.

The building, Arabic in architecture, reminds me of something the Moors would have built with white washed walls and arched windows. The windows on the second, third and fourth floors are each in a checkerboard style; in colors of burnt orange, Tuscan yellow, Earth brown and olive green. The building is boxy and square and taller than the other buildings next to it and gives the impression of having a fourth floor.

The regent, walking behind me, climbs the steep steps and we go through a door and into the darkness. We stand still for just a moment as our eyes adjust to the darkness and I climb holding my dress as I go up stairs that twist to the left each time we meet a landing.

As we ascend, I hear people talking on the second and third floors and I feel as though this is some kind of meeting place for the town's people. I reach the fourth floor, as indeed there is a fourth floor, and notice three arched windows open wide with the early morning spring breeze flowing in.

The room is large and empty with wooden floors and plaster walls and wooden columns that must measure 3 feet wide holding the roof. I walk around the columns then walk toward the windows and as I do, I can hear my shoes echoing on the wooden floors. I look down onto the streets below. People are working in their shops, talking amongst themselves and bidding good day to one another as horses pull carts laden with wares or food.

Something is about to happen. I'm waiting for someone. As I focus on this feeling, I sense it's a man, a knight, coming from another country. At this thought, happiness and love encompass my heart then just as suddenly anxiety begins pressing in on me from all sides. I turn to my constant companion, my regent, standing behind me. I can feel his cold stare boring into my body with such contempt. I return his stare with annoyance. The regent is a bone thin man wearing a fur coat that has openings for his arms to go through and his spidery fingers forming a steeple in front of his chest. His long nose and thin face are not appealing to me, in fact I find him quite repulsive with his ingratiating manner and his obvious desire to impress. I ask him, in a language foreign to me,

"Is this the right place?"

However, I understand every word as I speak it. He excuses himself to inquire and at last I feel I can breathe without his constant presence. He returns, enters the room with a condescending smile and tented fingers and informs me with a slight bow that yes, this is indeed The Three Kings' House.

I turn and look out the window once again and I see my reflection on the window pane. I am blonde and my hair is braided into a bun. The bun is placed in a hair net and on top of my head is a headdress. The shape is a large doughnut roll covered in the same satin material and color as my dress and golden braids crisscross around the roll. I wear simple pearl earrings that match the necklace I wear. In my reflection, I see clearly an expression of worry and in my dream I recall wondering when will he come? This was my last thought.

Chapter 1

OUT OF THE DARKNESS comes the light. At the beginning of time this was written. The Bible says, "In the beginning God created the heavens and the earth, and the earth was without form and void; and darkness was upon the face of the deep and the spirit of God moved upon the face of the waters and God said 'Let there be light' and there was light."

Even in the darkest black hole there is a fraction of light just as there can be darkness in the brightest of light. We need a balance of both. But what does it mean to find the light within us as humans, as individuals? Where was my light? How could I get out of my darkness and what was my purpose? This was the issue I struggled with so long ago.

So I began to ask people I knew, family and friends and even people I didn't know. They all gave different answers.

One said, "It's the shadow self."

Another said, "Work on the negative aspects of your character."

Yet another said, "Work on knowing thyself."

I was getting answers, but the one thing I realized was that every answer, even though worded differently, really meant the same thing and that was working on my ego, but how to go about this? That was the big question.

Then, one night I started having lucid dreams. I would see the essence of me dressed in clothes of a different period of time or as a different gender, but it was still me just wrapped differently. I began to write these dreams down; however, I never gave them a second thought. Trying to work on myself had to come second because just trying to raise my five year old son was a daunting challenge in itself. My day to day life would take all of my time and something as necessary yet as exotic sounding as finding my light would have to wait.

Several years passed with the blink of an eye and I found myself with two boys, a job I hated and a marriage that was coming apart at the seams. Coping each day became close to impossible. If there was any light within me it was the light of a guttering candle. The darkness was wrapping itself around me like an anaconda and squeezing the life out of me.

I had to find my way out of this inky blackness and no one was going to help me. I complained, I whined, I cried and I found fault with everyone. I had become a plague to my friends and family and no one liked talking to me on the phone. And who could blame them? I wouldn't want to talk to me. I didn't even want to be around myself. I went to doctors but I refused to take drugs for my depression.

They sent me to a psychiatrist and this didn't help. I realized psychotherapy wasn't working for me when I asked my psychiatrist a question and he didn't answer. I looked up from the couch to see this man with his headphones on and his eyes closed. He hadn't heard a word I'd said. I don't think he even realized that I had left the session. So, paying a doctor out of pocket was not going to work for me. I needed to help myself, by myself and apparently without his help.

During this time, I started having very lucid dreams again, seeing myself as another person. I wrote these dreams down the best I could, but I dismissed them as my subconscious trying to work through my conscious issues. Maybe I just wanted to be someone else.

At 28 years of age I had 2 boys and two jobs. I was divorced and wishing I wasn't alone to carry the entire weight. In one of those quiet moments when the kids were asleep and I was actually free to relax and listen to music, a song by Gilbert O'Sullivan, *Clair*, came on the radio and I was transported to earlier days. I began to see myself as a little girl of 4 or 5 running through the yard, picking yellow daisies and rolling in the emerald colored grass.

Life was so simple back then, was it not? No worries, no bills, no cares, but it occurred to me quickly that life was not so easy then. It really wasn't, at least not for me. I had so many fears as a child and growing up was not easy at all. Watching my own children sleeping, I knew it was not easy for them either. Changes happened and their lives were interrupted.

I've never tolerated change well. I fight it. Even as a little girl change scared me to the point of depression and almost despondency. It devastated me and the only comfort I could find was hiding under the bed in the dark. When my mother had a heart attack, I didn't understand what had happened. I hid under the bed. When someone was angry with me, I hid under the bed. When we adopted my sister, I hid under the bed. I was afraid of anything changing in my young life. This aversion to change only seemed to intensify as I got older. If I could have fit under my bed, I would have continued this pattern. However, now I would hide under the covers.

A thought crossed my mind as I sat there with my memories. I remembered writing in a journal when I was 8 years old. A second grade teacher, whose name I have completely forgotten, told us how writing our thoughts down would be helpful in relating to our past experiences as we grew up. It would be similar to "A time capsule in words." I begged my mother to buy me a journal and after 3 weeks she finally did. It was nothing special, a beige, faux leather book with *Journal* written in gold leaf on the front of the book. The edges of the paper were in gold leaf, too. I was very proud to own this journal being that it was my first journal ever. I would write my thoughts down, but each day sounded the same, nothing out of the ordinary. Then I decided to write my dreams down. I had such unusual dreams. Surely they would provide some colorful reading to my journal. Many of the dreams were kept in a file in my mind from the time I was 5 or could remember them. Where was that journal now? I started thinking back to when I first married and the possessions I took to my new home with my husband. Then it was clear, my mother gave me a box with old childhood treasures in it. It was outside in a storage shed! I quickly put my shoes on and went outside taking the keys to unlock it. The shed was small, messy and covered in dust. Trying to find that box was going to be difficult, but I was determined to find it.

It took me most of the day but I found that old beat up box. I brought it inside and began to slowly search through it. Pictures of school friends, drawings, arts and crafts and heart shaped valentines came out of the box. I carefully laid them on the table. At the bottom of the box lie my journals. As I took them out, I counted 10 journals. I had added, through the years, to the original. How could I have forgotten about all of these precious journals? All of this time, they were in the shed rotting away. But why would I have thought about them? They were written in a time I wanted to forget. I wanted to sit and read all of them but there was not enough time in the day. The kids needed to be fed and bathed and on to bed and so did I. It would take an entire three weeks to make time to read these journals.

Source: King James Bible, Genesis 1:1

Chapter 2

THE JOURNALS HAD BEEN lying on my dining table for two weeks, begging for attention and it was almost palpable. It seems there were always obstacles keeping me from them. I have heard that divine intervention comes when change is imminent and growth must be explored. Timing. I was about to be hit with providence that would give me the time and force me to look at my journals.

With the birth of my second son, there were complications. With great joy there are sometimes great obstacles and great pain. I think it's how we manage the obstacles that matter. I was diagnosed with uterine tumors. I was unable to ignore the pain and had one option: Removal. No woman wants to do this, to alter herself in this way and there are all of the stories to contend with. I wasn't the most pleasant of people at this time. Would this make me unbearable to be around? To say I was apprehensive and afraid would be an understatement. Was I going to lose everything that made me feminine? How would it change me? I was on that mental loop again. That loop of everything that could possibly go wrong and nothing that could go right. If I could make a tape and play a mental loop of only positivity, I would have. I had the support of family and I was allowed to heal fairly comfortably. I was living on painkillers and lying around watching television and in my own zone. I was a zombie of sorts.

I remember getting up and slowly making my way to the kitchen for a drink. I realized my journals were still lying on the table in the same place I had left them, undisturbed and slightly dusty. The books seemed to be alive and staring at me. In my altered state they had taken on a life of their own. I missed my boys and the quiet was a bit unsettling. I took this opportunity to finally delve into the Journals.

I grabbed my drink and the journals and slowly made my way back to the bed. I plopped the books on the bed and crept toward the window. I pulled back the curtain and looked out. The sky was lead grey and heavy with snow. Soon, snowflakes began to fall and when they landed, they looked like small pieces of cotton landing on the snow from the day before.

Inclement winter weather; I have always loved it. Everyone has a season, mine is winter. I know it's not so wonderful if you have no place to call home. Nothing is beautiful when you have no money, no home, no hope, and no perceived options. The most beautiful beach on the most beautiful day can seem cold and unwelcoming. However, I was sheltered and comfortable, slightly numbed and watching the snow fall. It was winter. I was in my element. I had the place, the time and I had no more excuses not to read the journals.

I put my drink on the dresser and shuffled my way back to bed. After fluffing the pillows, I grabbed the first journal on top of the stack, plopped down on the bed and began to read. I moved my hand over the weathered brown cover, over the word Journal written in fancy gold cursive. I gently opened the torn pages stained with age and it occurred to me how much I wrote like my older son. Reading the misspelled words written in thick pencil, I noticed I had only written about day to day occurrences and for only a week, which was strange because in it seemed longer in retrospect. The same thing, over and over again: Went to school, had lunch, talked to my friend and came home. I really didn't have an imagination at that age. Then like a magician looking for a spell I found what I was looking for. In between the pages about my daily routine, there were a few pages that were blank. I kept turning, and then I found the first pages about my dreams. Four dreams in particular. Each section was at least three to eight pages long front and back. I noticed much more detail in my writing. This must have been important to me back then.

Even at that age, it seemed as if I was writing mini novels. I relaxed and sunk deeper into the comfort of my bed. I turned the delicate crispy pages of my youthful ponderings until I got to the section I wanted to read. It's strange how we write when we are children. The sentences are to the point and more like reports, very staccato and nothing in chronological order. Some words misspelled or never written as we try to put the message down as quickly as we can. It was difficult to read. The memories of those vivid dreams came flooding back in Technicolor®. I read four of the dreams I had written when I felt I had to stop. The memories were so strong, I had to catch my breath and grasp what I was reading.

The dreams had been reoccurring ones. I had penciled in the number of times I had these particular four dreams at the bottom of the page. What leapt off the page were the line marks down at the bottoms of the pages, each in a different color: Pencil, blue pen, purple, red, black, and, sometimes green. I must have been keeping track of these dreams for a long time. I noticed this because the spelling of notes on the bottom of pages began to improve as I read on. Then it occurred to me that I had been looking at these journals and going over them throughout my adolescence and making a note of the number of times I had these dreams. My memoirs stopped abruptly. I realized, as I read on, I turned sixteen and began to work saving for a car. What a shame I didn't continue writing. Then I looked at the last two journals. These journals were written when I was in my early twenties. So I did continue writing about my dreams. I must have put all of my journals together at one time for safe keeping. How amazing that I was dreaming so vividly and so much. The dreams repeated and continued, however, in different landscapes and time periods that I didn't exactly recognize, yet I was vaguely familiar with.

I remembered the dreams and as the days passed the writing in my journals became more intense. So vivid were the colors that I wrote down as I detailed the dreams. I bought books on dreams. Somehow the interpretations they wrote in the books could not explain my dreams. Nothing matched up, so I gave up. What was all of this about and why did I feel so desperate to learn and uncover the answer? How would I solve this riddle? The riddle of the dreams.

Chapter 3

I HEALED, RECOVERED QUICKLY AND was back at work. My kids were back at life and things went on as usual for the next year, but there were many nagging unanswered questions. I continued to return to the dreams. They were never far from my mind. Always there, vying for attention. I went back to the dream journals, but that's about as far as I got.

The nightmare. I saw myself being taken away from my family and children. Then I saw myself being burned alive. I woke screaming and confused in pure panic. I ran to check on my children. Thank God they were asleep. Safe and sound and nothing was wrong in their world. What made me dream such a horrible dream? Little did I know that this was only the beginning of a nightmare that would continue to find a permanent place in my mind, my life and my being. Months went by and I was deprived of sleep. I felt like I was losing my mind. I couldn't concentrate on work. I had become obsessed. I had to delve into it. I had to know why I had these dreams and what they meant.

At that time, I was living on caffeine and cigarettes. Sleep, what was that? I had forgotten how to sleep. I had to stay awake, at least I felt as if I had to. I was driving in my surreal, caffeinated sleep deprived state, thinking about the dreams. I again began to have the same reoccurring dreams and night terrors. The fears and terror of my dreams were a reflection of what was occurring in my life at present. I had a fear of losing my children, fear of poverty, fear of heights and fear of dying a horrible death. Fear of success, fear of being alone and unwanted and unloved. Fear. How destructive is that?

Nothing made sense. I had finally had enough of this roller coaster ride from hell. I needed answers and I wanted the answers quickly. So I confided in a friend. The first person I thought of was Lyn. She had an open mind. She was constructively honest and never harsh in her remarks. We spoke briefly on the phone and agreed to meet. We met for coffee and I gave her the journals along with what I hoped was an understandable explanation of what had been happening to me. In return, she gave me some herbs that would help me sleep. She agreed to read them and let me know what she thought. I included two new journals containing all the nightmares I was having at that time.

Lyn told me not to worry so much; she would help me in my quest for answers. She gave me directions on how to make the tea, a quick hug and she was gone with my precious books. The books! They were gone, out of my sight. As much as I trusted her, I started to panic.

Driving home I began to doubt myself. Maybe it was wrong to let her take the journals. Maybe I should have given her only one. I started to worry that maybe Lyn wasn't as open-minded as I thought. I doubted my ability to judge character. Again, fear. If it had been anything else….. but the journals? Of course, she never gave me any reason to doubt her. It always mattered what people thought about me and I never wanted anyone to not like me. I do admit; I still get this way from time to time, but not as often as I did then. I was losing sleep then, I was going to lose even more sleep now that I had just planted these seeds of doubt in my head. The seeds were well planted. They were growing and in no time at all, my mind would drive me to distraction.

For the next two weeks, I was moody and paranoid. I found it hard to do my job at work. I wanted to call Lyn to ask if she had read the journals, but I was afraid of her reaction. Does she think I'm insane? Am I insane? Is she too nice to tell me I need a little trip away for some rest and relaxation? I was coming apart. I was sitting in my cubicle under a thick, black cloud and the phone rang. It was Lyn. She said "Can you come over after work?" I have someone you need to meet." Oh no. Who did she want me to meet? All I could get out of my dry mouth was, "Yes." And, we both said good-bye and hung up. These irrational fears. Where did they come from and why did I have them? Why was I so afraid to share the journals?

A volley of thoughts came rushing at me. What was I thinking to have given her those very personal journals? They'll take my children away. These thoughts were running through my mind on a loop, fast and furious. My hands were shaking and I felt ill. No, I was ill. I made it to the restroom just in time.

Was it normal, this abject terror? Why was I so frightened? It didn't feel normal in any sense of the word. This was almost phobic. I splashed water on my face and tried to breathe. I looked at myself in the mirror, the portal. I saw my reflection turn into a surreal series of events. I saw myself in medieval garb, a flash of a long past memory. I saw myself being taken away from my home. My children were screaming and crying and they too were being taken away by a man who I can only describe as an evil presence. I was being taken away with my hands tied in ropes and a rope around my neck.

As suddenly as this vision came it left, and I was in a white tiled bathroom looking above the sink and into a mirror again looking at my own reflection. Memory or vision. I really didn't know at that point. But the feelings were so real. I was going crazy. I was sure of that. My heart ached with sorrow and loss. My children. What made such a thought pass through my mind? The only thing I knew was that memory/vision was real. It was visceral. I could touch it and it did happen. I could feel it and it was real.

Chapter 4

THE DRIVE OVER TO Lyn's was nerve wracking. I took several deep breaths then I sat there in silence. After a while I began to realize I was being ridiculous. I got back on the road trying not to hyperventilate.

I drove on to Lyn's house, a beautiful Victorian home surrounded by other homes equally as lovely and all with flower boxes hanging from the ornate windows, The Historic District. Driving through and seeing all the beauty, the ancient trees, calmed me somewhat. I pulled into her driveway. Her car was the only one I could see. I took a deep breath and walked up to the door. She had a spring wreath hanging on the door and you could see where the birds had been trying to eat the decorative berries. I knocked and she answered with her usual enigmatic smile. "Come on in," she said with a wave of her hand. She gently touched my arm and guided me in.

We walked into the front room and I drank in the smell of fresh flowers. Lyn looked at me with casual yet concerned eyes. I assured her I was fine, yet that was far from the truth. "I want you to meet someone that I believe can understand what you've been experiencing." I walked into the living area and seated in an oversized chair was a small bald man. He was dressed in robes of yellow and red. He smiled and when he smiled, I felt that he silently conveyed that he understood my fear, my apprehension.

He slowly got up, and in one fluid movement, came to me and shook my hand gently. There was energy behind him, around him, and moving to encircle me. The energy was palpable, beautiful and reminiscent of all that was achingly beautiful. A feeling of peace and love overwhelmed me. Have you ever been in the presence of someone whose energy was so light and vibrated at such a high level that it made you cry? Tears were starting to feel heavy and I feared they would fall soon. He recognized me and I him. Lyn introduced both of us and I found out at that point that he was a Tibetan Buddhist monk. I was relieved and confused at the same time.

His name was Lepkana and with his broken English, he greeted me and sat down folding his legs. Lyn had been a practicing Buddhist herself for the last three years. The Temple was not far from her house. We all sat down and made ourselves comfortable. Lepkana took a drink of water and cleared his throat. Placing his glass of water on the side table he looked at me and smiled. I felt reassured and more confident when he did. I felt the stress from the weeks prior start to evaporate. He began to speak and even though his broken English was sometimes close to incomprehensible, I received his message clearly. His voice had a soothing cadence almost like music.

"My dear child, do you know what all these dreams and nightmares are about?" Do you understand them?" I sat in silence, feeling kind of goofy like the Grasshopper to the Master. I realized he was waiting for an answer.

"No, not really, but I do feel like my dreams are important somehow." A smile from Lepkana stirred me. His dark, chocolate colored eyes twinkled. A flash of Santa Claus bearing gifts crossed through my mind.

"You have had these dreams since you were a young child, from what Lyn tells me." I looked at Lyn and Lyn looked back at me with understanding. I shook my head yes, in reply.

Lepkana said "Do you know about past lives and what they mean to us as humans in this life?"

I was a little taken aback with this question. I didn't expect it. He could see my confusion, but waited patiently for my answer.

"I have heard about past lives but I was raised Catholic. They don't believe in past lives. Catholics believe in Purgatory."

He smiled then laughed a laugh that sounded like a child's. He cleared his throat again and spoke.

"My blessed child, what do you think you have been dreaming about all these years?" My eyes moved from him to the carpet below me then back. I was perplexed, my mind changing gears, trying to comprehend.

"I just thought they were interesting dreams. Possibly, more... I really don't know. You're telling me that I have been dreaming about past lives all this time? Is this normal?" He laughed that innocent laugh and clasped his hands together. "Yes, I am! I am telling you that from what I have read in your journals, these are memories of past lives, and yes this is normal, whatever normal is for you. But of all the individuals of the world that I have met, I have never met one who has had them as often as you."

I never left his line of sight. He smiled slightly but at the same time he was serious, his comforting eyes watching my every move. "Your past lives are about drastic change that has affected you in this life time and placed fear in you."

He took a drink of water and spoke softly this time, "Change happens, it comes at you like a lightning bolt and tosses you around like a raging sea, then a calm comes for a while and sometimes only for a while. You can only change what you can, but we can always strive to make a positive difference."

I looked over at Lyn, She smiled and touched my shoulder letting me know in some small way I was not crazy and that I was going to be alright. I looked back at Lepkana, "Do you still dream of your past lives?" he asked.

I replied, "Yes, but not as often as I did at one time. I guess other things occupy my mind, like my children, work, you know, life in general. They haven't stopped completely" My thoughts drifted for a moment. It occurred to me that I had a past life dream a couple of weeks ago, more of a past life nightmare. I had written it down in my journal. My attention turned back to Lepkana. "Does a person stop dreaming or having visions of their past lives as they get older?" "Well it all depends," he said. "I guess it would be up to the individual. You have free will. You can continue to dream about past lives for as long as you want to. Tell me about your dreams. Tell me in as much detail as you can. I'm very interested to know more."

At this point Lyn came in with some herbal tea. I hadn't even noticed she had left. She poured the tea in cups and passed them around. I took a sip of mine and began to talk. "Well, these past life dreams are always vivid, always in color. Even on gloomy days within my dreams, colors pop up. I have seen people that I know in this life time but in the dreams they are not the same. What I mean is they don't look the same. Different hair, different sizes and shapes, color of their skin, etc. Even though they look different I still know them. It's like I can see into their soul and know instinctively who they are. Do you understand?" I asked the quiet monk.

He smiled and nodded his head, and situated himself more comfortably in the chair, as if he were getting ready to watch a good movie. Even Lyn got comfortable. This was all too unbelievable. Here I was telling this holy man about my past lives and he really wanted to hear these stories of my life before.

I continued. "Their faces change...I mean in my dreams, the people. Many times I see them shift back and forth, going from who they are now to who they were at that moment." He looked at me somewhat perplexed. "It's like watching someone shape shift from past to present. Does this make it clearer for you," I asked nervously. "Yes, yes I understand what you are saying, please continue."

"I feel, sometimes, like I'm watching a movie about myself. Many times the dreams are very detailed; I can even smell the smells from that time period." My heart was racing at this point with excitement. Having the chance to tell someone who I knew would never pass judgment on me for what I was telling them gave me a sense of relief. I have seen myself die in different ways and different circumstances and I have also seen how others have died and that's when a deep stillness and sadness came over me. I was quiet for a moment.

My thoughts drifted to a past life dream I had only two weeks ago about my youngest son who was my daughter in that particular lifetime. I remembered my daughter/son screaming and running after me as I was being taken away.

I heard a cough and this brought me back to the present and I noticed Lyn and Lepkana looking directly at me. I felt somewhat embarrassed for wandering off. "Oh, where was I? Yes I was telling you about what I have seen in my dreams." Lepkana looked at me in a way that made me feel he knew what I had been thinking about. He smiled back with understanding and compassion. If he only knew how difficult it was to talk about the dreams... visions... these past life experiences that seemed so very real time to me.

"I feel everything in these dreams: Happiness, sadness, pain, anger, depression, hate, love, judgment and so much loss. I can see every detail from buildings to mountains; fields of flowers in bloom at spring. These dreams are so real I could have touched these objects and they would have been solid. At times I'm a third party and at times I am the person interacting with others. I have reoccurring dreams with the same beginning and end. I instinctively know that these types of dreams are vital and important, but as to the reason why, I have no idea."

I drifted off again trying to answer my own questions in my mind. Trying to figure out what all of this meant. I realized the room was silent. I looked up and Lyn and Lepkana were waiting for more. I felt a little awkward, so I cleared my throat and spoke.

"What more can I say? You've read my journals. You know all that I know and maybe more than I know." I looked at Lepkana. "I do have a question." "Go ahead, ask away" Lepkana said in a kindly manner, almost melodic. "I find it difficult to grasp that I'm having past life dreams. Are you sure this isn't the result of a wild imagination?" Lepkana looked at me and said, "From what you've told me, what I've read and what I feel in my soul, you have been dreaming of your past incarnations. It's clear to me that you chose to remember who you were before you reincarnated into this life. I think it's quite possible that you have been dreaming of past incarnations since you were an infant. By the time you were four or five you began to remember and found these dreams strange and different. This is your soul helping to acknowledge that these dreams are not normal dreams but dreams from a distant past. Buddhists believe in past lives, but we also believe that we should fix the issues and move on. Have you ever been to these places or seen pictures of these places before dreaming of them?" I thought for a moment, "No -I have never physically been to any of the locations I dream about. I have seen pictures but only after I've had the dreams repeatedly. For example: I had no idea I was dreaming of England, Scotland and Wales or even Ireland. When I was a teenager I saw pictures of these places, the villages. I actually felt homesick for places I had never been to in this life time."

Lepkana and Lyn were silent. "Many of the dreams are in unfamiliar countries, and I have no idea where they are and I speak different languages in my dreams. The only languages I know are English,

Spanish, Italian and some Greek. The languages I speak in my dreams are not any I have spoken in this life and I'm confused by that. I know about Karma. Is this Karmic? Do I have so much to make up for? Was I really such a horrible person in those times?" An understanding smile crept upon Lepkana's small face. "It is not for me to judge. It's only for you to learn and understand how much you have changed. We all must learn from patterns we continue to make in this life time. It is the acceptance of what has happened if only to move on from fears that hold us back. Fear keeps us blocked and slows our path to enlightenment. When a person lingers in their past from past lives or their current past it's only because the individual cannot let go. They have not forgiven themselves or forgiven others, they hold on to all of the ill."

Lepkana said "I don't feel you lingering. There is an important reason for this phenomenon to have been happening to you all your life. Maybe out there somewhere, there is someone who has had the same thing happen to them. But to be honest, I've never heard of past life dreams occurring so regularly and beginning at such a young age. I have no doubt that you will find the answers in time."

I fell silent for a moment until Lyn got up from where she had been sitting so quietly. I had forgotten she was even there. I looked up and Lepkana was getting up, too.

"I have to go now." He walked up to me and held my hand.

"I'm sorry I can't stay any longer, but I have a class to teach. This time with you has been most interesting. Please come join our classes for meditation. I think this will help you. Do you meditate?"

"No…I don't know how. I've tried but I can't stop the chatter in my mind." I felt awkward telling him this. He held my hand a little tighter. "Then I will teach you. I wish you the very best in your journey." He put his hands on my head and gave me some kind of blessing. Touching him gave me a strong love for, well, everything and everyone.

I couldn't help myself, I touched his shoulder and he turned. As unaccustomed as this Buddhist monk was to embracing anyone, I hugged him and he laughed and hugged me back. I felt like crying. His clear energy had such a profound effect on me. It was pure, well as pure as I had found and, loving and graceful. For some reason, I felt like I would never see him again. I had no idea at the time that this would turn out to be true.

Lepkana left for England a few days later for a celebration the Buddhist have there, a celebration of Love and Compassion for all. This Holy man gave me so much wisdom and love and compassion in the span of one day. He literally changed my perspective on life. He left this life on a journey of his own one night while in England before the celebration. His journey had taken him to Shambhala where all enlightened beings live. He went home.

Chapter 5

I DID AS LEPKANA RECOMMENDED. I went to the classes and learned to meditate properly. It was difficult at first, quieting the mind. After a few months I found that I could quiet the noise in my head and be at peace; wonderful, blissful silence. I did the chanting and found that it gave me energy and awakened my soul. I started practicing Buddhism. I was finally seeing a change in myself, a change for the better and the past life dreams were not occurring as frequently. I was happier and kinder and more loving to others. I had peace within myself. Then, as we often do, I let the material world come rushing in like an ocean wave crashing on the beach and washing over me, making me lose all balance, and I began to forget what I had learned and what made me happy.

Three years passed and I noticed, during this time, that people I met or worked with seemed to have some type of connection to me. I also noticed that all my old fears were creeping back in. I thought I had worked this through, but in reality, I really hadn't. The meditations were great but I wasn't working at the core of what was causing the fear. All the chatter came back. Life started to lose its luster.

I started dating Nick; I met him at work, Nick Reed. Although, I had never met Nick prior to working with him, there was a viable yet vague connection there. We both wondered when and where we had met before. Actually, we realized we had met in more than one past life. As soon as we started dating there was something unsettling about the situation. Even though I felt that I loved him, I felt that he didn't exactly share my feelings, but I would always send that to the back of my mind.

I had low self-esteem and no confidence in myself. I was working two jobs and stressed out. In two months time he lost his job and was about to lose his apartment. He asked if he could move in for a while. He didn't want to move back home with his mother. Who would? Reluctantly, I let him move in with me.

The first two weeks of cohabitation were peaceful, but then he began acting differently. He preferred to be alone and would take my car leaving me stranded. That's when the dreams began in earnest. I began to have dreams and visions of us together in an ancient time. I was a Roman High Priestess in a temple for healing. He was a Roman soldier who had come to me for healing from physical and emotional pain. He began to recover and soon we became lovers and this was forbidden. He had bewitched me and seduced me for so long that I gave in. He began to pressure me to leave the Temple and live with him as his wife. I wouldn't do this; I had given myself to the Goddess I adored. This enraged him to such a degree that he came to forcibly take me away. Before he could do this, the alarm was raised and he was captured. He told the courts everything about us. He lied and twisted events and accused me of bewitching him causing him to love me. The courts believed him and I was subsequently sent away for disobeying the laws, but not before being beaten by my elders, each taking a turn. Then I was put on a boat and cast out to sea with nothing but the clothes I had on. They expected me to die but in the dream I survived. However, I became ill and died a few years later. I felt as if I had died of a broken heart because everything I had ever known was taken from me because of my stupidity and because of this man's obsession with owning property...me.

I woke up in a cold sweat, barely able to breathe. I looked over to where Nick should have been, but he was gone. I got up and washed my face and went out to the living room where I found Nick chatting with on old girlfriend online. We exchanged some harsh words and he denied that he had been talking to her. The dreams came, almost as omens, warnings about him, warning me to remember him and his betrayal in the past.

The next dream involved a similar situation with the present/past - Nick pursuing me in the middle ages. As in the first dream, he only wanted me because of the land I held as an owner in a time when women did not, as a rule, own property. In this vision, again, I was a healer. I had a child – a girl from a previous marriage. I had no idea that "Nick" wanted only my property. I really thought he loved me. He proposed marriage but I said no. I really didn't want to marry.

My land was protected because of the court papers my husband had filed before he died. At my refusal to accept his proposal of marriage he became outraged. I was heartbroken over his anger and I knew then all he wanted from me was what he could gain materially. Shortly thereafter, five men on horseback arrived and accused me of being a witch stating that a person to whom I had administered healing had died. I knew this wasn't true. I had not practiced healing on anyone for many months. I began to scream and shout at these men, "No, you are wrong!"

Face to face with my accusers, one of the men hit me full force with his fist. I heard the contact of his fist on my face before I realized it had actually happened. Bones crushed and skin tore. This man was beating me and as the blood poured down my face, I heard him call me a "Filthy bitch." All of this in front of my ten year old daughter, holding a pan of feed for the geese. She dropped the pan and ran to me screaming and crying and begging them to stop. They were set on taking me away. My daughter pleaded as she tried to get closer to me. What could a ten year old girl do? I was more concerned with the horror my daughter had to experience. Then I saw "Nick." Not his name in the dream, but clearly him, on a horse in a field watching everything. I knew he had conspired with these men. He was responsible. My eye began to swell shut and my nose was broken. My lip was torn open from the blow to my face and I was removed promptly.

My trial followed only two days later and I was found guilty of witchcraft by judge and jury, liars all. People I had healed and nursed back to health. I was sentenced to burn at the stake the next morning. I had precious little time, but I found my thoughts were with my daughter. What would happen to her? Where would she go? Had they hurt her? I never saw my daughter again in that life. My property was given to the man responsible, Nick. This was a horrid dream but I knew deep down it had happened. I knew it was happening with the same person in my present life.

He left after my insistence; he had no choice. I found out he had been seeing someone else and stealing money from me. I was heartbroken, not because of his actions, but because of what happened in the past. Had I learned nothing from these past lives? I became deeply depressed. I needed to find out more about these past lives and why I was starting to meet more people that shared the past with me so long ago. There was a pattern starting in my life that would continue.

Like many single women, I had two jobs. My second job was working at a dinner theater. I worked there from the mid 1990's until almost 2001. I had gotten to know several co-workers quite well and found some friends among them. One in particular was Krista. She was open-minded with a very generous nature. She taught me everything I know about calligraphy art. She's one of the best calligraphers I've come in contact with. We got closer and I felt comfortable telling her about my past lives. She suggested a hypnotherapist and I searched for the right one. I found a woman who came highly recommended named Jeanne Rose Mill. She was giving a group past life class at a college and Krista and I went. I had never been hypnotized and neither had Krista.

We were both apprehensive about going but also excited to find out more. Jeanne explained about Karma to the class of twelve and she went on to say that our past lives have to do with Karma and fears, blocks and programs that we have taken with us as we incarnate to another life. Good Karma/bad Karma or maybe some people owe us Karma and they are making up for it. Confusing. How you could tell which past life dealt with fears, blocks, programs or Karma? I was intrigued. She explained that you would have to look at the past life dream or vision you were having and how you felt at the time. What happened? What was done to you? What was the trauma? For example: If you have killed another in a past life and you met them in the present, this would constitute as Karmic. You would owe them for taking their life. Jeanne also went on to explain how we could heal our past lives and not dwell on them but benefit from the experience. I started to understand.

Krista and I went through the entire hypnotherapy session with the others, but I was uncomfortable being in such close proximity to so many people. Later, after class was over, Krista and I went and spoke with Jeanne. She was more than willing to answer our questions. She told Krista and I that she could sense we had been sisters in a previous lifetime and had come back to meet again as friends to help each other out. Was this the reason I had become so close to Krista? Jeanne gave us both a business card, but before we left, she said to me, "I can see that you will start meeting many more people from your past and whether this is good or bad I really don't know. You will also start recognizing places that you have seen in your visions. Just go with it and see where it takes you." I stayed there staring at her for a moment, then Krista broke in saying "We should go." I had no idea how true Jeanne's statements were and how instrumental the people who came into my life would be in helping me grow into my own truth and finding my life's purpose. My journey had begun.

Chapter 6

I RESEARCHED EVERYTHING I COULD about past lives. I came to understand the difference between past life dreams and dreams that we have as our subconscious is trying to work through our conscious issues.

Studying past lives was and is fascinating. To understand past lives I had to understand other religious beliefs. So, I started studying and went to other churches to understand their practices. The religions that most interested me were Buddhism, Hinduism, Gnosticism and Paganism. Judaism interested me as well but more so the Kabbalah. Catholicism was infinitely interesting, but being raised in this life a Catholic, possibly I was a little too close to it and familiarity sometimes breeds contempt.

I was able to find some peaceful moments in which to meditate. At that point, I decided to devote myself to meditation once again to stop the endless chatter in my head. As I was mediating, the familiar stillness came over me. I felt my body relaxing as I began to breathe slowly. At that point a vision materialized and I saw myself as a little boy of about ten years of age with brown hair cut short almost to resemble the fringe of a monk's hair. I was wearing a beige shirt with the sleeves rolled up, short breeches with a rope tied around the waist to hold them up. The clothes were tattered and torn and mended many times over. I was standing on top of a hill and looking approximately 100 yards to my left, I could see a castle. I looked down from the hill at the village below in the valley.

The village was Medieval with buildings made of stone and mud. I could see the sun setting in front of me. I ran down the hill toward the left side of the village and came to a stone cottage where I could see the smoke curling upward from the chimney and when I opened the door I noticed how small the cottage was. As I walked in the kitchen, there were two open spaces further back that had one large bed and the other space had a smaller bed. Curtains covered the openings for privacy. My father was piling more wood on the fire and my mother was cooking and rolling bread onto a clean cloth. She placed eggs, bread, cheese and a jug of wine in a basket.

I could clearly tell she was upset about something and my father was very quiet. I knew they had been arguing with each other. The energy in the room was heavy and dense. I felt sad because I somehow knew they had been arguing about my grandparents who I think were my mother's parents. My mother spoke to me in a language I had never heard before, still, I perfectly understood what she was saying to me. She wanted me to take this food to her parents who lived on the other side of the village. I took the basket she gave me and with a kiss, she whispered in my ear to be careful. She told me to go in between the other buildings and to take a lantern that held a candle.

On I went, with my basket, to my grandparent's home. As I got closer and closer to their house, I became excited. I loved them very much. I knocked our secret knock and my grandmother opened the door. She smiled. She was so happy to see me and she looked around cautiously and gently took my arm and escorted me in. She called out over her shoulder into the other room. I knew she was calling for my grandfather.

My grandparents were old but not so old that they needed to be cared for. They did quite well on their own. Their house was very large compared to my parent's cottage; it had three separate rooms. My grandmother gently took the basket from me and set it on the table. They both gave me a big kiss on the cheek and a hug.

I saw from the corner of my eye something twinkle from the candlelight. I looked and saw a button of some type that had designs on it. It looked like it was made of silver or pewter. It had a large cross that separated the button in to four sections. On top of the cross was a circle then a smaller circle in the center. There was a flower engraved on the bottom left, then an X with small circles on both sides. Both top openings had circles and smaller circles all around it. At that moment, and without being told, I knew instinctively that my parents were Catholic and that my grandparents were what they called Bon Hommes, just from seeing that button.

After the dream and in my research, I found out that Bon Hommes meant the same as Cathar. Even though I instinctively knew my grandparents loved me, they were nervous, anxious and so were my parents. I knew my parents loved my grandparents and I saw this with clarity. As I stood there, a boy of ten, I knew that the Bon Hommes were considered heretics to the Catholic Church. The Catholics wanted to kill them for their beliefs. I also knew that my parents and grandparents had made a firm agreement with each other that if my grandparents were taken away, my parents would publically denounce my grandparents for my sake. I understood that it was for my safety. They were both doing this out of love for me and this made me feel so guilty.

I felt guilty for being alive in this time. Guilty for making the people I loved so much have to make a hard decision like this to save my life. The vision dissipated leaving me in tears. I had a feeling that my grandparents did not have long to live in that particular past life. Once I composed myself I knew who those people were in this life time. They were my grandparents in this life; my mother's parents. Now, I began to understand the incomprehensible guilt I felt every time we went to visit them even as a little girl. They both are gone but even now those memories haunt me.

The guilt is still there and even thinking about this makes my heart ache. At least there was no one in this life time coming after them to kill them for their beliefs. They lived a long life and saw so much in this world that they will carry in their souls to the next life. The place that they lived, in that sorrowful past, was a place called Puivert, France. I recognized the castle in the movie The Ninth Gate with Johnny Depp. I researched until I found the village and the castle ruins. The picture I found online was exactly the same as the village I looked down into so long ago.

Chapter 7

A s I was questioning my own actions and feelings from past lives, I realized that I did not learn from prior lives. I was repeating patterns that caused so much grief for me in this lifetime. Guilt with my grandparents, relationship patterns, fears and phobias kept me from progressing spiritually and emotionally. Regret settled deep within me, lingering for months. I was asking for guidance from God and seeking answers for expelling these learned and repeated behaviors that always ended in disaster.

Time went by, no answers came or maybe I just didn't see the signs. I was impatient, lost and living in regret and this is one of the worst places for anyone to be in. Days and weeks passed and my world began to look colorless. In the weeks that followed this depression, I began to sense a feeling of impending doom. I could not comprehend what was happening now or what was going to happen, but I kept my children close to me at this time in the event something serious did actually happen. What I did not know was that the apprehension I was experiencing was related to this vision. The days leading up to the next vision were eventful and weeks went by very quickly. I almost felt as if I was in a dream state.

I remember reading about stigmata and how before the sacred event occurred, the person seemed to be in a trance, euphoria actually, for days. Even smells of roses or perfume lingered around them. Then the sacred event of stigmata would occur and an intense suffering, feeling the wounds Christ felt on the same parts of their bodies when He was tortured and crucified. The grace of God would flow through them as tranquility returned. A deep connection to God, Christ and to the universe was made evident to them as never before. I knew a stigmata state would not happen to me, but fear of the unknown kept me awake nights.

The next day, I came home from work exhausted, took my shoes off and sat comfortably on the recliner. My boys, who had been home all day with the babysitter, asked me when I would prepare dinner and I replied, "Later, Mommy needs to rest right now." The boys left me alone and went to play in their rooms.

I closed my eyes telling myself I would rest for 20 minutes and then make dinner then proceeded to fall asleep as soon as I closed my eyes. I entered a dream state and in this dream, my heart was racing. I heard people talking and children laughing and I knew this was the continuation of a reoccurring dream that I had when I was a child.

The dream starts the same way: Darkness falls and I am on the slope of a mountain, near the top on which the castle sits. There are smells of a campfire and torches burning mixed with the scent of an earlier rain. I am at a campsite and as I walk around, I notice tall metal poles with crosses affixed to the top of them; the crosses have three round metal balls at each point. These crosses are placed in the front of one tent. As I pass the tents, I have a feeling that something of importance is happening inside these tents. I recognize the symbols. I begin to see other familiar symbols. Leather belt buckles in the symbol of the astrological sign Pisces. I know that this is the sign of Christ, "The fisher of men." Torch fires and the moon illuminate the campsite. Forest trees and bushes surround parts of the slope and on one side of the mountain there is a sheer drop off, almost vertical.

I walk toward a large bowl made of pottery made for catching rain water and place my wooden cup in the bowl to scoop up a drink. From the torch light and the moonlight, I see my reflection in the water. I notice that I am a young woman of about 20 years. I have long dark brown hair and the color of my eyes is green. I notice that I'm wearing a long robe that looks like beige wool. I have a rope wrapped around my waist but the rope is not to hold anything up, and as I run my hand over it, I realize it's a cord indicating my pledge to be a Parfaites.

I can hear someone yelling in French, but a different dialect of French. A man yells, "They are coming, everyone to the castle!" At that point, I hear women speaking rapidly in the same French dialect while trying to collect their children. I turn to see the women and children running toward the castle but I notice that the men stay behind and I then realized that they are going to fight the soldiers that are fast approaching on foot. There must be a thousand of them and it is almost a deafening roar.

In my dream, I was so frightened that I began to run toward the castle and that is when I noticed that the women and children had reached the safety of the castle and the huge wooden doors were slowly closing. I turned to look at the men who were trying to hold off the soldiers, but I saw them being cut down one by one by foot-soldiers armed with swords. It was too late. I would not make it safely to the castle. In this dream, I was observing as a third party. I was observing myself.

I ran as fast as I could to hide among the trees. I turned back several times as I ran to see the only knight, mounted on his horse, coming toward me at full speed. He rode a large, muscular black horse, and in that moment, I saw his black tunic with chain mail underneath. On the tunic, there was a large white cross. His greasy, shoulder length black hair was wavy and he had a crazed look on his face. As he was riding, his hair fell sloppily to the side of his face, yet his extremely well manicured and neatly trimmed beard and mustache marked him as a vain man. He was bearing down on me, his sword held out in front of his body. I ran toward the woods praying for a miracle to save me and save the others.

At that point; I knew the Catholic Church had finally broken through with their soldiers to kill all of the "heretics" and I was one of them. I turned again to see the knight crashing through the trees to get to me and there was nowhere to hide. I had reached the edge of the cliff. Once more, I looked back to see him getting ever closer and my last thought was that I would not give him the pleasure of killing me. Then I jumped. I closed my eyes as I fell straight down not wishing to see as I crashed among the rocks. I felt my body crush, every bone, as I hit the hard surface of the flat rocks. An excruciating pain electrified my body but only for a moment and then no pain at all; nothing, only darkness.

Suddenly, I glimpsed a small bright light. The light began to get bigger and bigger. I was in a tunnel of white light. The quality of this light was pure and warm; an overwhelming feeling of love radiated and made me feel as if I belonged exactly where I was. I wanted to walk into this light, this tunnel, and never go back.

Then, I heard the voices of children calling "Mamma, Mamma" and I woke up to see my two boys standing in front of me. I was back in the present. My clothes were drenched with sweat. Everything seemed surreal and I was trying to determine if I were still dreaming. I looked at the clock hanging on the wall in the living room and an hour and a half had passed. I took a deep breath and I knew I needed to write this vision down as I saw it. I knew this dream had important implications. This reoccurring dream had never completed as it did. I wrote it down, all of it. As I prepared dinner a little later than usual, I couldn't remove that picture of the man that chased me from my mind. I also had many questions about the religion I was practicing in my dream. I was sure that the tunnel of light and the blissful feeling of being complete and whole was a vision of entering heaven. I wanted to go back to that light and I wanted to walk through that tunnel to the end because I knew the end was heaven. At this point, I knew I would never fear death again.

Death is a transition, nothing more or less. If my boys had not awakened me, would I have died? Would I have continued on through the tunnel and beyond? I didn't know the answer to all the questions that were raised in this vision/dream, but I did realize that Cathar was the religion I practiced and it would re-surface over and over and over. I knew how significant that particular mountain and castle were. I needed more information.

Chapter 8

I WAS NOW ON A quest to research the places that were coming to me in my dreams/visions. I found the mountain and the castle. The castle is still there. It's now called Chateau de Montségur, and it was built on the ruins of one of the last strongholds of the Cathars. At the time, the Catholic Church's mission, according to Pope Innocent, III was to wipe all "heretics" from the face of the Earth. He reasoned that by doing so, the Catholic Church would be one step closer to eradicating any religion contradictory to their beliefs in his maniacal pursuit for total control and total power in the western world. They almost succeeded in this. The Cathars and other religions began to go underground to escape the persecution of the Catholic Church in their ceaseless quest for power and control.

Moving through the process of research was helping me to understand where these locations were and I found some explanation for my deep rooted fears and belief patterns that kept me in stasis and kept me from finding my own personal light. I must say, in my research, written histories of certain geographical areas were confirming all of the places that were connected and visible in my past lives. They did exist. They were real.

I was peeling off the layers one by one. I had more enthusiasm for life. I was finding the answers to my questions and the questions to my answers; I was on the journey I was meant to take.

Due to the dreams which led me to the research, I was intensely curious about the Cathars. At this point, a friend gave me a book called

The Cathars and Reincarnation by Arthur Guirdham. This book was monumental for me in that it explained the Cathar belief and way of life. A way of life I was intimately familiar with. The Cathars believed in a dualistic world. There were two Gods, one in heaven and one on earth. The Earthly God brought pain, sorrow and chaos to humans. The God in heaven knew our very soul and almost grieved with us as we walked this Earthly journey. The more I studied this way of life (never considered a religion) the more I understood my own beliefs and where they came from. I started to realize how all religion played such a grand part in control; control of the masses, control of ourselves, control of our basic desires. It's all about control.

We, as humans, have faults and failings and we do have a hard time finding light in a world that is so dark. This makes it possible for religion, of any sect, to settle into our reality. We think we need this guidance. However, the Cathars believed in looking inward and toward the soul for answers. They didn't need a confessional or a middle man, they could commune with the sacred when they chose by looking inward and realizing that all are one and one is all. If you hurt one, you hurt all, if you help one, you help all. There is a quote I once heard and the sentiment rings true to my heart: "Religion separates us, but spirituality brings us together..." or something to that effect.

Slowly, I was connecting the dots that caused me to behave the way I did and to believe the way I believed. All of the negative and positive patterns followed me throughout my past lives and into my present life. I realized behavior patterns were not the only part of my life that needed to be thought through and worked on.

My fears kept me from moving on and becoming successful in any endeavor I pursued, personally or professionally. Through my research, I realized my fear of heights stemmed from leaping to my death from the cliff at Montségur. In the brief moment, when I still had lucid thought, before jumping off the cliff, I realized I did not want my life to end in such a horrible way; running, afraid, being chased to my ultimate death.

Does anyone want to end this way? I had a choice. I could let this man run me through with his sword or jump to my death. I chose to have control over my own demise. I could not and would not let this person, this barbarian, this henchman, make that decision for me.

I knew, in the depth of my soul, that I would be back to begin a new life in a new time. I was confident of that. My soul would never die, only the vessel and I made my choice.

I still had no firm answers as to why I had these dreams/visions and where they would lead. Could all of these dreams/visions be the source of my irrational fears and phobias? Were they from past lives? Trying to figure out this entire situation and find some cohesion took a toll on me in my present life. I found myself dwelling on multiple past lives and the trauma arising from them. My quest for spiritual understanding began to fade away as reality, brutal and harsh, took over.

Footnote: Pope Innocent, III (1160 or 1161-16 July, 1216) was Pope from 8 January, 1198 until his death. His birth name was Lotario de Conti di Segni, sometimes anglicized to Lothar of Segni. Pope Innocent was one of the most power hungry and influential popes in the history of the papacy. He exerted a wide influence over the Christian regimes of Europe, claiming his supremacy over Europe's kings. Pope Innocent was central in supporting the Catholic Church's reforms of ecclesiastical affairs through his decretals and the Fourth Lateran Council. This resulted in a considerable change of canon law. Pope Innocent is notable for using interdict, excommunication and other censors to compel kings and princes to obey his decisions. The pope called for crusades against militant "heretics" like the Cathars, as well as Muslims. One of Pope Innocent's most critical was calling upon Christian forces to begin the Fourth Crusade. Although the Crusades were, in part, originally intended to support the Byzantine at Constantinople from attack by Turkish invaders, the Fourth Crusade resulted in the sack of Constantinople by the Crusaders in 1204.

Chapter 9

A FEW YEARS WOULD PASS before I approached the subject of my dream/visions again. There would be another man, who, unbeknownst to him, would help me find my winding way back to my past, present and future as they were intertwined like rope with three strands wound into one.

People walk in and out of your life. Some become close to you and others not so close. Some you would like to know better, but they may not like to know you better and that's okay. Working at a dinner theater was exciting yet stressful. I was living amongst actors and their props. Working there took me away from this life and projected me into another reality. Helping customers and seeing their expressions and noticing their anticipation of excitement made me wonder if they had past lives that reflected the time period in which I was working. So many people came to me and said they recognized me. Not all of the time, but frequently enough to make me wonder why they were asking. Strange, but life is strange, is it not?

One night, as the show was in progress, a manager and I were standing and chatting by the gift shop. The large wooden doors opened from the arena and we turned to see who it was. A woman came walking out, an average looking woman; nothing really stood out or grabbed my attention. The manager and I waved and said, "Hello." She looked at us in a peculiar way as if she had a taken a drink and that drink had left a bad taste in her mouth. We watched her walk into the women's restroom. I turned to the manager and commented "She must have had too many Margaritas." Suddenly, I noticed the manager stiffen up as he stared past my left shoulder. I quickly turned to find the woman that I had accused of being drunk standing right next to me. I stepped back a bit, composed myself and noticed she was staring at me with loathing and disgust and confusion all at once. It was as if she recognized me and wondered what I was doing in her world. She said, clear as day "You watched me hang! I know! I was there and I saw you!" This woman was angry! She asked me "What are you doing here!" She had accomplished her goal of intimidation and I felt her negative energy go up one side of me and down the other and then circulate.

Her words and her energy confused me. However, I composed myself and we were almost at pistols drawn and ready, we were at eyes locked. I saw her features change and she became a woman in her mid thirties. She was dressed in medieval garments with a white head scarf. I knew she was one of the people I had accused of being a witch. I knew that she was actually a midwife. In that past life she was a competitor and her disdain for me in this and the past life was palpable. I felt the same way. She was a threat to my status as I was also a midwife in the same village. Jealousy consumed me. I knew that she was more knowledgeable as a midwife than me and I wanted her out of the way… gone. I wanted to be *THE* village midwife.

One of her patients died and this was all I needed. I used it against her to prove an unnatural death. My accusations were taken seriously. Ultimately, I saw her on a scaffold with others who were to be hanged. I saw her family, her husband and her children. They were devastated. My eyes lingered on her family, and as soon as I turned around to look at her once again, the chair had been kicked out from underneath her feet and she was hanging.

At that moment, I was interrupted by the manager. He asked her to please return to her seat. She looked upon the manager and back at me and I could not speak. My throat was dry with the horror that I caused this woman. I was the accuser and had caused her death. She turned and went in the direction of her seat. I heard sotto voce, "Bitch." Could I blame her? No. I felt my knees buckle and my manager helped me to a chair. He said he saw all of the blood drain from my face and I was white as a sheet. He asked me, "What the hell was that all about?" I couldn't explain something to him that I was bewildered about. I tried and after a glass of water that he had given me, I told him I really didn't know what she was talking about. As I told him this, I couldn't look him in the face. I knew inherently what she was talking about. How could I explain this to him? He knew something was wrong, but he didn't press me further. I was visibly upset. I'm sure he didn't need the headache.

I was literally sick at my stomach with guilt and sorrow at what I had done to this woman. I had caused her death and ruined any hope of her family continuing to live in the village. They were shunned and cast out, unwanted. I did not wish such a bad fortune upon this family, I truly didn't. I just wanted them to move away from the village and to stop interfering. However, it all went wrong and it got away from me. It was all due to my selfishness and jealousy.

Chapter 10

A NEW CO-WORKER WAS TRANSFERRED to my theater, another manager. They transferred him due to his acting and managerial skills. He was very, very handsome with chiseled features, hazel eyes and long blonde hair. Yes, quite handsome with an extraordinary physique. There was an electric quality to the air when I was in his presence. He was charming with a generous nature. To look at him, you would think he would be a bit arrogant or full of himself; however, this wasn't the case with him. His name was Caleb.

Caleb moved to my area with his live- in girlfriend and we became friends and he confided in me. We had many long conversations about varied subjects. After three years working together, Caleb and I were asked by upper management to come in and decorate for the Christmas holidays. During the time we were decorating the Great Hall, he asked me aside to talk. He asked for a ride home. When we were through decorating, we hopped in my car and I drove into the rainy night toward his house. He was very quiet on the ride at first. Then he stunned me by telling me that he was in love with me and had been for the three years he had been working with me.

When you meet a true soul mate, it can wreak havoc on your little world. He was a true soul mate and it was like standing on top of a high building with floor to ceiling windows. I felt the vertigo and the dizziness and my heart raced as he spoke. I was confused. He began to tell me his deepest thoughts. He said he knew me, "I know your soul." I felt as if I would have an out of body experience and found that I had to pull over to the side of the road to compose myself – his voice seemed very far away and as if in a tunnel and I was in the tunnel with him. Safely off the road with the rain pounding a tinny rhythm on the car, I looked into his eyes and past life recall occurred at that moment.

I saw us in a country manor home in England. We were together in the home, but I was not his wife, I was his mistress. I felt that distinctly. He had provided this home for me and our children, two small boys. I felt the pain and sorrow of loving this man, but not being able to be with him publically as his wife because he was married to another. This wasn't some kind of line. There was a connection and he was bringing it to my attention. He did love me in that time, absolutely, and when he spoke about it, chills of confirmation covered my arms as he was trying to convey this to me.

I returned to a conscious state of mind and I was in the present, in my car with him. I wondered what had just happened. Time and space, past and present melded and mixed at the same time. There was no difference. He touched my face and turned it toward him and asked me if I recognized him. "Don't you remember me?" he said. Even though we had never confided our beliefs about religion or past lives, I knew he understood and he had been to the same places I had been. Why had I not recognized him when I first met him? Why did he have to repeat the same words he had spoken so long ago for me to realize who he was and who we had been and what we had been to each other?

We drove to his home in silence. I was still stunned by his revelations. Before he got out of the car, he told me this: "I want you to be with me. I don't want to be without you." I had the feeling that he meant to say, "I don't want to be without you…..again."

Weeks went by. I knew that I couldn't be a mistress, not again. Even though he and his girlfriend were having problems, I couldn't put myself in the middle no matter how badly I wanted him. Not again. I had to learn not to repeat past transgressions and mistakes even if this meant we couldn't be together in a relationship, not in this lifetime. When I gave him my answer I tried to convey these feelings to him. He would have to be alone, single, available. It couldn't be the way it was the last time. I saw the hurt in his eyes at this response and he looked crushed. I couldn't understand why my co-worker/friend would have such a strong reaction. I started questioning my own feelings and beliefs. Had I really known him before? Is that even possible? I began to think about the Karma that it would cost to have a relationship with this man.

I was trying to rid myself of negative Karmic energy at that time. It didn't work in that lifetime and it wasn't going to work in this lifetime. I decided to remove myself from the situation, place, everything. I wanted him to be happy. Everyone deserves happiness, even me.

It took the situation with Caleb to make me realize just how lonely I was and how much I needed to give and receive love. Why is it always so complicated? I'm not talking about fairy tale love, but love that has no boundaries, no expectations, and no limits. Not someone who wants to change or mold you into a version of their ideal. But, how can anyone love you when you don't really love yourself?

There is one thing I do know... real, unconditional love never dies; it follows you into the next life and by some divine hand it comes back to you. What you do with your second, third, fourth chance is entirely dependent upon the circumstances of your present situation and how you choose to deal with it.

Chapter 11

IT'S FUNNY WHAT LONELINESS can make you do. Loneliness throws you into a place of desperation; it is a feeling that no one should ever have to feel. Getting rid of this agonizing feeling involves occupying your thoughts and that's what I did. My routine consisted of two things: Work and children. This was my antidote, my drug. But it never really gets rid of the lonely feeling you have. Because, when all is peaceful and the children are asleep, that's when you can be found sitting alone, sipping your Earl Grey and reading a book about….what else…love.

Everyone I knew seemed to have a relationship or was meeting someone. It made me sick and jealous to see my friends so happy. I wanted what they had; holding hands, laughing and those subtle, sensual glances that lovers share. Maybe this feeling was inspired by watching too many movies, yet I wanted to have something special with someone. I wanted to be at an al fresco Parisian restaurant doing the dance, flirting. As cliché as this sounds, I was wrapped up in the romanticism of it all. Or I could be real with myself and know that I had no idea what real love is, much less flirting with a hot guy on a warm Parisian night. Where is Paris anyway?

My self esteem and confidence spiraled downward more than it ever had before. There was no lover in my life and at this point and I really didn't think he was coming any time soon. I was angry with myself, God and everyone else. Everyone else except me seemed to be lucky in love. Why did I have to see the past life I had with Caleb? Was it real or was it a fantasy? Actually, it was real and it did happen, just not in this lifetime. I knew I had been dreaming about past lives since I was a child of five or even younger. Was it really me in those dreams? Now, I began to wish I'd never had the past life dreams.

I began to doubt the visions because all they did was cause so much pain and sorrow and I felt cursed. Being made aware of these past lives took a heavy toll on me; physically, mentally and spiritually. I was losing sleep thinking about Karma that I had neither confronted nor healed from. But where did I begin to find the Karma that I had created in the past?

The very next day, I went to a bookstore in seek of yet another romance novel. Looking around, I found a section called "New Age." I was scanning the bookshelves when I came across a section dedicated to Karma. One book in particular caught my eye. As I pushed books around to find what I was looking for, an audiotape fell on the floor quite by itself. If this was meant to get my attention, it did. I picked the audiotape up and read the title, *Karma Releasing* by Doreen Virtue. As my Italian/Spanish grandmother would have said, "Un segno di Dio," "A sign of God." I bought the audiotape and took it home; however, I didn't listen to it. I left it in my dresser drawer and didn't play it until after Christmas of that year.

I think, looking back, I was afraid of facing my ego and my ego was afraid of facing the truth. There was a huge fear factor there. The universe aligns and synchronicity happens and it was about to happen to me.

Chapter 12

THE CHILDREN AND I were invited to Maine for a vacation by an old friend of mine, Diana. Unfortunately, it was past Christmas and well into winter and we missed the beautiful changing of the seasons. The house itself was situated on a rock outcropping in Seal Harbor. Very well kept, but a little weathered by the brutal Maine winters. A very imposing old home; white with a dark green steeply sloping roof. Wrapped around the front and sides of the house was a large white porch and there was a cupola painted white against the green roof on the north side. I could just see a woman from times gone by waiting, walking and watching for the ship that would carry her lover home to her. As I was imagining this scene I could almost hear the sirens of the sea calling in a lonely, haunting song. Watching the snow falling onto the roiling ocean was beautiful and I felt lonely looking on by myself. I found myself wishing someone were there to share the moment with me.

I snapped back to reality when I heard the happy voices of my sons as they ran up the stairs to the house. Diana's boys and her daughter we're running down to meet us all.

After dinner, we decided to go see a movie. We packed the kids in the car and Diana and her husband and I took off for town. At the concession stand we ran into an old friend of Diana's. He was about 5'11", blonde hair and brown eyes. He seemed a little mysterious and when he looked at me as I shook his hand, it was as if he knew me. I introduced myself and as he paid for a coke, Diana whispered, "He's divorced." He was seeing the same movie we were and we sat side by side. We seemed to do more talking than watching the movie. At that time, I didn't know that this new acquaintance would turn into a two year, on and off relationship; a long-distance relationship. He lived in Maine and I didn't. He was a business man and he traveled and also worked from home. Sometimes he would come to me and at other times I would return to Maine to see him. This arrangement seemed to work for a while, but he soon wanted more. He loved Maine and wanted me to move there with my children. My boys were getting older and they were established at school and I wouldn't take them away from their friends and their activities.

After about a year of this arrangement I noticed a change in his personality. He was quick to anger and he had outbursts. Growing up in the era I did, I recognized the signs of a drug problem and he definitely had one.

I went to Maine on one of my visits and as soon as I got off the plane and into the car, I noticed that he was aggravated. Aggravated that I was even there and it just got worse. It got very uncomfortable. During the weekend, my eyes were wide open and I noticed just how deep into his addiction he was. He disappeared into the bathroom constantly and he became very controlling, just nasty all around. It was a nightmare. I made a quick escape and I knew I had to make a decision. My children had been shielded from his craziness and I couldn't deal with it anymore.

During this time I went to a friend's house who had invited a psychic over to do Tarot readings for her friends. The psychic's name was DeLaney. She had a business card in elegant, silver script – **DeLaney.**

By this time; I had already seen several psychics so this was nothing new. Everyone had their turn and some had expressions of happiness and some seemed upset. My turn came and I went in to a private room in my friend's house. Incense was burning, candles were lit and there was a large crystal ball on the table. The tablecloth was purple satin.

De Laney was in her mid sixties with dark brown hair and gray roots, very skunk like. On every finger on both hands were silver rings with gemstone settings of various shapes and colors. She had been a beauty, French Canadian possibly, I thought. I saw a beautiful face that would have stopped traffic at one time, but was now ravaged by hard living or drinking or maybe tragedy...I really didn't know. She asked me to sit down. Her voice was a mix of whiskey rasp and smoke. She cleared her throat and started to shuffle the cards. I noticed that they were worn from time and use and I could tell that they had been a good friend to her. I shuffled the cards as requested and cut them three ways to the right. She took the cards I had just cut and spread them into a half circle and told me to pick 13 cards and think of a question. I asked about the situation I was having with my drug addled boyfriend, even though I couldn't believe I was even thinking about him. I was still trying to give him the benefit of doubt and I was concerned for his welfare.

She flipped each Tarot card over and laid them out in a cross in front of her and the other cards were around the cross in the form of a circle. She focused on the cards and looked up at me. She said, "You're in a relationship that's Karmic." I looked at her curiously and said nothing. "This man owes you Karma, *so* much Karma! He did a terrible thing to you in a previous life." I said, "What terrible thing!" She went on to say, "You were a High Priestess to Hathor in Egypt and he was a Roman soldier, a very high ranking soldier. I see him then as a very selfish and controlling person. He loved you; however, he was not in love with you. There is a difference – do you understand this? He wanted you as a possession. He doesn't understand the difference between love and lust. He didn't then and still doesn't. He has worked through a lot of faults and Karmic debt, but now he needs to focus on the present Karmic energy, the energy that exists between you and him. In that past life he gave you an ultimatum." The very word, "Ultimatum," stunned me.

She started speaking again. She told me, "He wanted you to make a choice between your religion and your way of life or him. In that lifetime, he wanted you to accompany him to Rome, but you refused. You didn't want to leave your position as High Priestess. You didn't want to leave the Goddess. *No* one refuses a Roman soldier, but you did. To put it mildly, he was angry. He went to the Temple of Hathor where libations were being given for that day and he took his knife and stabbed you. He stabbed you from behind through the right shoulder blade and into the heart. You fell at the statue of Hathor. I see blood running in rivers beneath you. As you died, you had no idea who killed you. I see him turning, his red cloak sweeping and with a twist and a smile that would make the strongest of people cringe, he walked away from you, quickly." She looked up at me and she said, "You still have the mark. It's a dark grey or black spot on the upper part of your right shoulder blade. It's been bothering you for a while, hasn't it?" A quiet "yes" escaped. That was my only response.

I asked her what I could do to fix the Karmic bonds. She told me that he has to fix his own Karma and I would have to forgive him. She said, "When that day happens, the Karma will be over for you and for him and there will be no need to mend Karma between the two of you and you need to understand this." She continued. "Well, you need to understand that he did a shameful thing out of greed and lust. He killed you in a Holy place and this is sacrilege. You were bound to Hathor and this caused his action to be cursed. Both of you have to fix this Karma in this lifetime! The next will only be worse if you don't."

I understood the Karmic connection and the tether that held us together in the present life and in the past. I would have to do some soul searching. As damaged and broken as our relationship was, we *were* bound together and we would be together in yet another life until the Karma was healed. "Forgiveness and understanding – people make things so difficult."

Chapter 13

THINGS HAD TO CHANGE. First on my agenda was ending the relationship with my Maine man. I needed a sense of purpose, a new career, more education. I loved helping others so I looked into the medical field, but which way to go? There were many options. I looked into nursing, therapy, nutrition and found nothing gratifying there. I started to get frustrated. I really had no idea which direction to take.

I came across an ad in the Help Wanted section of the newspaper advertising for Surgical Technician training while I was at work, on break. I called and made an appointment for the next day to speak with a counselor. I filled in all of the paperwork for grants and loans and I was accepted into the Surgical Technician training program. Soon after being accepted, I quit my job working at a mortgage company. I was excited and happy about being accepted. I had money in the bank and got a part-time job to subsidize my expenses. This all happened in the month of July and I felt that I had accomplished a lot in a very short period. I noticed an increased level of energy and more confidence.

I started school at the end of July and the classes were very interesting. I could foresee that this career would give me a sense of prestige, a sense of worth and excellent pay for the rest of my working life. I had found my niche, my happiness. Even in this happy state of mind, I still worried about the Karmic ties that were keeping me tied to Maine and my sadly addicted friend. My ego and I were doing fine without his drama/trauma because I was creating my own drama in my own reality.

When ego takes over we have a tendency to become self-centered with no consideration for anyone else. Pissing people off became an everyday reality for me. I was working toward success and having a good career as a surgical technician. I was intent on making a better life for myself and my children. I wanted my sisters to treat me with respect. I wanted everyone to treat me with respect. I was tired of being kicked around (EGO). I didn't want my children to be ashamed of me. I wanted to provide a better life than my parents provided for me.

Many times we *think* we have life worked out and we are on the right path, on top of the world. The reality is that no matter how high we are flying, we are not living in a way that encourages synchronization and a natural, organic flow. Once again, the universe steps in and it becomes clear to you that you were never on the right path; you were following the ego and not the Spirit.

The universal Creator has a weird way of letting you know when you're not on your path and when you've gone south one too many times and veered too far away.

My sign came in the form of a gold Saturn running through the intersection and directly into my path. The speed limit was 35 MPH and I was going at about 38. As I was approaching an intersection at the top of a hill, green lighted and headed straight, a Saturn in the opposite left hand lane stopped. We looked at each other briefly and he hit the gas. I was still moving and we collided in a major way.

My car hit his passenger side door full force, enough to move his car sideways. This was not a fender bender. My airbag deployed and the firing mechanism caused the airbag to catch fire. I still have two large round burn marks on my stomach. A passerby put the fire out with a large cup of iced coke. My hand went all the way through the windshield and I had no idea my left hand and arm were mangled. I was taken to the hospital by ambulance, admitted and there for 24 hours. My car was totaled. As I was lying in the emergency room I had an epiphany; why was this happening to me at this time? I realized that I had not cut those Karmic ties and it was wreaking havoc on my life.

Wake up call. That accident stopped me from furthering my education and I lost my part-time job. I lost a lot. But, I would soon find out that this was just the tip of the iceberg.... I would lose even more.

I was on the way to losing everything. I lost my car; without a car I couldn't go to school or work. The dominoes were falling. Two days later a police officer called me to tell me that the man, the other party involved in the accident, the man who took the wrong turn and changed my life, was at the time of the accident, legally drunk (way over the limit). Drugs were found in his car, Valium, Xanax, Vicodan. His car was full of open beer bottles and he was drinking a beer when we collided. The officer told me, "He was wired for sound." She also informed me that he was out on bail after being arrested and she said, "I'm sorry to tell you this, but he has no insurance. I suggest that you get an attorney as soon as possible." I could hear more dominoes falling, clack, clack, clack.

After arranging to have photos of the injuries taken at the police station and viewing his field sobriety test, I went back home and I fairly fell apart. I had one paycheck left to pick up and that was all that was between me and the street. As much as I hated to ask, I called everyone I knew. They were all busy with their own lives. I had given when help was needed from me and I really thought someone would come through for me. That wasn't to be the case.

You know, I've been depressed just like anyone else. I've been down. This was dark and way deep down. I wanted to lock myself in my room and stay in the dark. I was questioning why this was happening to me. I was doing everything right, wasn't I? Going to school, trying to improve my situation... but, my motives were not right. Ego was leading me and when you lead with your ego, you're living outside of your true soul and your true being. No matter what you do, if your motives lack integrity and you're not being true to yourself down to the core of your being – there is no Universal connection. Without this connection, you merely exist, you don't thrive.

I felt as if I was having every negative emotion and thought. It was a rainy, grey and uninspiring day. I gave up on my dreams. If I lost the house, if I lost everything, well it just wasn't meant to be. I made up my mind, that day, to surrender. As long as I had my boys, nothing else really mattered to me. I...just...let.....go.

The phone rang. It was an attorney from M.A.D.D. She told me that the driver did indeed have insurance, he had lied. At the time I didn't know that accidents involving suspected drunk drivers are routed to M.A.D.D. She went on to say that she would take my case. "I don't have any money to pay you." I said. She said "Honey, I get paid when you get settled and I get ten percent. Do you have bills that need to be paid, do you need anything?"

Certain cultures, Native Americans, for example, believe in Totem Animals. They believe that when you see a Totem Animal, a swarm of butterflies or dragonflies, it has great significance. I borrowed a car and went to see the attorney the next day. As I drove and exited off the toll road going up a hill, out of nowhere hundreds of large, orange and black Monarch butterflies surrounded my car and they followed me off the toll road and then started to disperse. People slowed to watch this amazing sight. I was mesmerized by it. Butterflies mean transformation. This doesn't happen every day. When you surrender and you let go of your ego and you become more selfless, miracles happen. I let go and I surrendered and I got my confirmation, hundreds of little flying confirmations in the form of one of God's most beautiful creations.

After seeing my attorney, I regained hope and I knew that everything would work out just as it should. It *would* be alright. I picked up my two sons that night. I had been holding onto every penny tightly. That night we splurged! We went out to eat Mexican at our favorite place. A simple thing, I know. But it was caviar and Champagne to us that night. Our caviar was Mexican food and our Champagne was two rental movies! Things really were going in the right direction.

Three kings House also known as The House of Three Magi - Trier, Germany the building I saw in my dreams. This building was established in 1230

A Cathar coin or button probably used by Cathars to recognize one another during the eradication of Heretics

Carcassonne France the fortified village. That could possibly be dated back to 3500 B C as settlement at that time for trading goods. The fortified city became famous for the Cathar Wars and a place of protection for the community of Good People

A medieval painting of the Albigensian Crusade

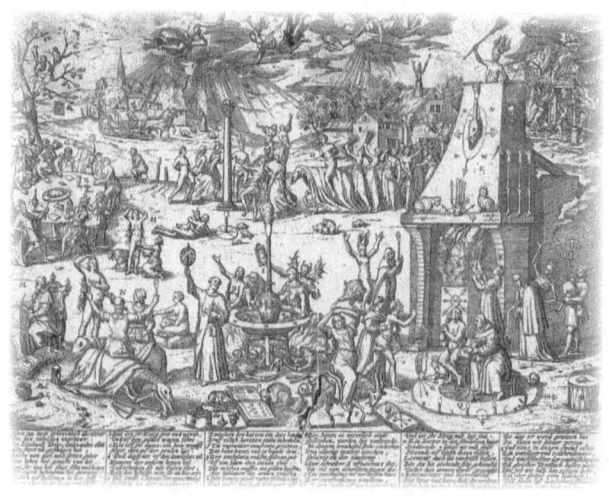

1594 pamphlet of Trier Witch Trials

Chateau de Puivert which had links to the Cathars and Troubadours

*Pope Innocent III pronouncing the Confirmation of
Rule to the Franciscan Monks. Pope Innocent III was
the Pope who created the Albigensian Crusade to rid the
Catholic Church of heretics in the South of France*

*Cross of Trier placed on the square during
the time of the 1594 Witch Trials*

Chateau Montsegur that lies on the top of the Pog (meaning mountain in Occitan language) the last fortification of the Cathars

A picture view of the village of Puivert France

Chapter 14

FOR THE NEXT THREE weeks I worked around my broken and cast arm. I went back to school to try and re-enroll, but I was not fully functional and not able to do the tasks required. I could start again next semester.

On Thursday of the third week after seeing my attorney, I walked out to the mailbox and noticed a dragonfly going by. As I had my hand on the door of the mailbox, I saw a cloud of dragonflies coming my way; blue, green and red. All sizes. They surrounded me and even landed on me. I watched this phenomenon for a while. I felt aware of my connection to my soul. I was on my own path and not worried about proving anything to anyone. My heart was opening and I was on my way to being in the right place, connected to the All. By the way, dragonflies bring the light and color into your life – it signifies change, another sign.

I opened the mailbox and found a letter among the bills. It was wrapped around a check for six thousand dollars from my attorney. Written in the body of the letter was "Here's some money, go get yourself a car." It was signed by Serena, my attorney at M.A.D.D. So, I got a car! A red Nissan 300 SX for $3,800 and I had money left over to cover some bills. This was in November. I was able to provide a big Thanksgiving dinner for my boys. We thoroughly enjoyed it. I was able to buy Christmas presents. Things were good.

The second week of December I had an appointment to see an orthopedist and the news was not good. Because of the hasty operation in the emergency room (not done by an orthopedic surgeon) all of the tendons and ligaments in my left arm that were damaged in the accident were treated improperly and I would never have full use of that arm again. I had no insurance at the time. The orthopedist told me that a surgical glove would only make my hand and arm numb and I would drop instruments. I had been going to school to be a surgical technician. That was no longer an option. This put me back in worry mode, but I realized after a couple of days that I needed to have faith. Everything truly happens for a reason and I believe this.

Christmas passed and the New Year came. My boys and I spent a quiet New Years evening at home watching the ball drop in Times Square on television.

I went back to meditation, working on clearing Chakras, rehabbing my arm and walking to lose the weight I'd gained. I wanted to detoxify my body, mind and spirit. January passed and February came. Money was low and I was still waiting for the settlement from the accident.

Serena called me the second week of February. "They want to give you $80,000." This was too low, way too low and I told her this. I heard her say, "Rat bastard." We were both in agreement about the lowball offer and she told me she would go for as much as his insurance would pay and that was $200,000. So, that's what we did.

Chapter 15

AN OLD FRIEND CALLED me one day, quite out of the blue. Jacqueline. She said "I have a proposition for you. My Uncle, who used to be a professor of Medieval Studies, has a colleague on the East coast and they're both doing studies on alternative history. I've told him about you. They want to get a team together to go to Europe. The downside is that you'd have to be there for about a month and a half." She said the flight and accommodations would be paid. I would need personal money for gifts, souvenirs, etc. I thought what personal money? I was slightly intimidated about being with professors. I didn't have their extensive formal training, but what the hell, go with it.

Alternative History.... I really wanted to talk to this professor. I met him at Denny's. As I sat down across from him, he asked me to call him Greg. Even sitting he was tall. He was a slender man with graying hair. Judging by his attire, clothing was not the most important thing on his mind. He jumped right in and smiling he said, "Let's talk about medieval history." He asked me what I knew about religion in medieval times. I had been researching the Cathars and I told him about some facts I had learned about the more than 500 religions of that time. We went from Queen Elizabeth I to the Crusades of Jerusalem. We spoke for about 2 hours. I'm fascinated with this subject so the time passed quickly. My job would entail research in Europe, church records, visiting libraries, and documenting architecture photographically - even talking to the locals about customs and history.

My group would meet promptly at 7:30 each morning, have breakfast and separate into small groups to hop trains, buses, trams and even planes in our quest to gather research about alternative history; the real story. He told me we would cover the areas of Southeast and Western Germany, up into Saarland and into the Austrian border, then Paris for a few days and on to the South of France to work and have a two day break, then off again to Vienna and Salzburg. I was excited about the South of France. However, Germany caused me to feel a bit apprehensive.

We shook hands before parting and he told me his partner, Dr. Lansky, would be in contact with me soon, as would he.

A few days passed and I received a call from Dr. Lansky. In a flat, monotone voice he asked me a few questions; my personal thoughts about religion and history. I told him I was open-minded and very curious especially as to why there were so many religions and separate beliefs during that period when the Catholic Church was so dominant. Also, history fascinates me. Why do we keep repeating the same mistakes over and over? We never seem to learn the basic fact that those who don't learn from history are bound to repeat it. I said, "It just never seems to sink in." He agreed. After 20 minutes, he said, "I've got to go. Greg and I will be in touch." I didn't hear real commitment in his voice so I told myself, no big deal. As soon as I have the money, I'll take the trip myself. I would go to Europe on my own expedition, swing back and get my boys and take them on a 2 week vacation, but I needed a passport and I realized I didn't have one single suitcase. The next day Dr. Lansky called me and asked if I could be packed ready by the third week in May. It was the last week in February.

Another week went by without word from Serena. I started to get a little nervous. I had approximately three hundred dollars in the bank. The passport alone would be one hundred dollars. I started to list all of the things I would need for this trip. Would I need to borrow money? I had the standard bills to pay and nothing extra.

Synchronicity. As I was making my list and wondering how I could afford this trip plus pay my bills, Serena called, "Surprise, Surprise! When do you want to pick up your check? We didn't get every penny, but we came really close." I think I actually screamed. Yes, I'm sure I did.

I picked up the check two days later, deposited the money and started in earnest making the arrangements for a journey that would lead me down roads I never, ever thought I would travel. Naturally, I felt guilty about leaving my sons, even though they would be well taken care of. They were thirteen and nineteen at the time. I hadn't been this excited about anything in a very long time. They knew this and encouraged me to go.

I checked rechecked and checked again.... suitcase, passport, ticket, money. I just wanted everything to be perfect. I have to admit that I was a little afraid of going on my own. This was my first time abroad.

The next day, I woke at 6:00 AM to get ready and be at the airport by 8:00 AM. The boys, my ex-husband and I all went to the airport. I hugged and kissed the boys good-bye and left them with their father. As I went through to the scanning procedure at the airport, I looked back one more time and waved good-bye again. My heart ached. I would miss them. I had never been away from the boys for more than a weekend. This would be for a month and half. I would be alright and so would they.

Finding my seat was easy. But the take off was going to be a little hard. I knew that take-offs and landings are the prime time a plane could crash. These thoughts were on my mind. The lady next to me must have noticed how tense I was. So she began to talk with me, asking where I was going and for how long. She was German born but lived in the States for forty years with her retired military husband. We were so engaged in conversation and I hadn't even noticed that the plane was already in the air. I turned to look out the window and saw the tops of houses and the green parceled bits of land as we headed up into the clouds and I started to relax.

I must have fallen asleep. Stretching a little, I scanned around to see that some people on the plane where watching a movie or reading a book; some were asleep. The German woman was not in her seat so I assumed she had to be in the restroom. I looked at the flight plan on the screen in front of me and I realized we were just crossing over into Nova Scotia. Soon we would be flying over the water. Gladys, my German seat mate, had returned and was settling in her seat when the plane made a terrible jerk. I heard a few people scream from somewhere in the back. I grabbed my seat belt and locked in. The plane jerked again, worse than before and a few overhead compartments on the other side opened, throwing passenger belongings in the aisle. Now I was scared. I looked at Gladys and said, "What's happening with the plane?" She had a worried smile on her face. This wasn't making me feel better. "Just turbulence... that's all," she replied. Then the plane shook violently. I thought it would break apart. Suddenly, I realized we were over water. I started trying to come up with a plan on how to survive. I couldn't think of one. Then the captain came over the intercom. "Ladies and gentlemen, we are experiencing some strong winds as we are trying to get the plane over the thunderstorm at this time. Please have your seatbelts fastened and stay in your seats. Thank you." The captain's voice didn't reassure me much.

Flight attendants came clanging down the aisle with the drink cart. This was the quickest I had seen them move since I had been on that plane. Gladys asked for four Jack Daniels bottles, two cokes and two glasses. She looked at me with that worried look and said, "This will do the trick!" As soon as she said that, the plane jerked and heaved and lightning struck next to the plane. Gladys gave me two bottles of Jack, one coke and a glass. If we were going to die, I was going down with a drink in my hand. I opened the first Jack bottle poured all of it in my glass and opened the coke and poured just a fourth of the dark sweet liquid into my glass. Then I drank it down just like a shot. Opened up the next bottle and did the same. After downing a few Jack and cokes, Gladys and I didn't care if the plane crashed. We were so numb we wouldn't feel much.

I was awakened to noises of coughing and babies crying. I had been having a nightmare about planes almost crashing into water. I looked at the seat next to me, Gladys was snoring peacefully. The other passengers were getting up and going to the restroom or just trying to stretch. I looked at the flight plan in front of me.

I noticed we were passing over France, getting closer to Frankfurt, and I could see the sun rising. Gladys who was so much help to me on my first international flight went through customs with me. I spoke no German, not a word of it. She guided me through the process and we hugged and went our separate ways.

Chapter 16

PICKED MY BAGGAGE UP and met Dr. Lansky and his wife who were waiting for me outside the baggage area. Dr. Lansky grabbed my luggage, hefted it into the back of his silver mini-van and off we went to the hotel in Frankfurt. Dr. Lansky's wife, Maria, did not seem like a very happy person to me. Possibly, she didn't care for Germany. I really wasn't sure. Just something I picked up. As we were driving, Dr. Lansky was going through the itinerary with me, but I started to drift away and his voice began to fade. There was something so familiar about Germany. The structures and buildings, even the air, and all the colors evoked memories. The colors seemed to be much more brilliant than the colors I was used to.

I snapped back to listen to Dr. Lansky just as jet lag was really starting to hit me. I needed some rest, but I didn't see that happening any time soon. He wanted to jump right in and get going. We arrived at the hotel and I met all of the people I would soon be working with, including Greg, milling around in the café and the lobby.

My luggage was being taken up to my room and I heard Maria talking rapidly to Dr. Lansky in Hebrew. She seemed flustered and somewhat angry. There was one more person to be collected at the Frankfurt airport. I got the impression that she wanted Dr. Lansky to pick this person up personally. That he was someone of importance, at least to her.

I finally made it to my room and managed a shower. Even that was difficult in that jet lag fugue. I hit the bed and woke up about 3 in the afternoon. I got up and went to the windows. I opened the French doors and stepped out onto the balcony. The air was fresh and cool. I was on the seventh floor and I looked down and all around and got my first real view of Frankfurt. For the most part, it looked like any other city, but in another country. It was great. I left the windows open, the air was sweet. I called my boys and then got ready to meet the rest of the group at 7 PM for dinner in the hotel restaurant.

On my way down in the elevator, it stopped on the fourth floor. This was my first meeting with Jenny and her husband, Pablo. We exchanged introductions and had a short conversation on the way down then went together into the restaurant where we met the others. I noticed another person had been added to the group, the last person that Dr. Lansky picked up from the airport. He looked to be about 5'8" and he wore a Yarmulke. He had a short military haircut. He vibrated disdain. I felt that he was in a quandary as to why all these non-academics were in his space. Our little rag-tag group of researchers. He stuck very close to Maria and Dr. Lansky, more to Maria. He made no attempt to be friendly or introduce himself. Greg was sitting by me and he leaned over and told me this man's name was Amasa, Maria's cousin. Little did I know at that time that Amasa would only last three weeks. This is when I started to pick up on a feeling that something other than just research of alternative history was going on. As I said, it was just a feeling I had.

During dinner we received our written itineraries outlining the geographical areas each to which each group would be traveling. Jenny and Pablo, Hans, (the German student), and I would be going to Saarland. Dr. Lansky, Maria, Amasa and Greg would be going to Berlin. The rest of the team would stay in Frankfurt.

Dinner was delicious mix of roasted chicken, fried potatoes and salad. After dinner, Jenny, Pablo, Greg and I went to the hotel lounge for a drink. Greg picked out a wonderful tasting red from a German vineyard not far away from where we were staying.

Relaxed, conversation flowed easily. Rita mentioned that she would like to visit Dachau, so Greg told her that he would try to arrange it. He also warned her of the ghosts that inhabit Dachau. He asked her if she'd ever been and she said, "No." His description of Dachau was very interesting. He said that his experience, when he visited the concentration camp, was a feeling of deep sadness and he wanted to cry. He said, "No wind blows there, but when it does, it chills you to the bone." His wife was unable to finish the tour with him. The mood turned after the Dachau discussion. We finished our drinks and wandered off to our own rooms.

Chapter 17

I RETURNED TO MY ROOM, windows still open, the fresh air still drifting in, I slept through the entire night on a Swedish bed without moving. I woke at 5 AM completely refreshed. I started the coffee and enjoyed it on the balcony watching the sun rise. I took a shower and got ready for the next phase of this adventure.

I met my group at 9 AM. We left the hotel and walked about half a mile down to the train station. It was evident, even from last night that Hans, our interpreter, was going to be more of a problem and less of a help to us.

At the train station, Hans got his ticket and started to walk to the platform to board the train.

"Hey!" Pablo said.

"Did you forget something? You're supposed to interpret for us."

Hans turned to Pablo and told him to get the tickets himself. "I'm not your keeper," he said. Pablo found a train attendant who spoke English and secured tickets for our group. The train attendant said, "Are you going to the same place that guy's going?" indicating Hans. "Yes." Pablo said. She rolled her eyes.

We made our way to the platform and boarded the train bound for Saarbrucken. This was my first train ride. Jenny sat to my right, Pablo across from her. I had a window seat and an empty seat in front of me.

Hans chose to move as far away from the group as he could. He was a few rows up from us. The train started and we were on our way.

Ancient villages started passing by my window and I realized, as an American, just how old everything in Europe was. They don't raze the old structures as we do in the United States. I could almost see things as they were in the 1500's or 1600's. The history of these places...I could sense it, see it, smell it just as it was.

I think it took two hours to get to Saarbrucken, but I was so absorbed in the landscape I didn't notice the time. We were pulling into the Saarbrucken platform before I knew it. We got off the train and Hans told us he would take us to our hotel. When we arrived at our hotel, an unassuming but comfortable place, we unloaded and then headed to the Historical Records Building in Saarbrucken. My task was to look up the medieval religious history of Saarbrucken. Greg wanted a breakdown of religious sects: Protestant, Jewish, and all religions practiced from 1100 to the early 1900's, an interesting task that took all day. And, for the next three or four days, we were there working on our assigned duties.

Later that night, we had dinner at an Asian restaurant. The food was good. As we were eating, Hans informed us that we would be going to Trier the next day. I said, "Trier? Where is that?" He told me it was up the Saar River which meets and flows into the Moselle River. Hans told us that Trier was the oldest city in Germany. Trier had been an established city since 1300 years before Rome. At various times in history, Trier had been inhabited by the Celts and the Romans. It was a medieval city. The buildings were still intact and true to the era. Interesting!

How exciting to be going into cities I had never heard about. We checked out of our hotel the next morning and boarded the train heading to Trier. Once again I had the coveted window seat with Jenny sitting next to me. We seemed to be riding parallel to the Saar River.

It was a beautiful emerald green. I noticed steep hills, more and more of them. There were vineyards and buildings at the plateau of these hills. It was beautiful, more than beautiful. We passed ruined castles and castles that were being restored and being used. There was a village every 5 miles.

Looking out the window, I remembered what my Dad once told me: Of all the countries he had been to as a Staff Sergeant in the Army, Germany was the most beautiful place he had ever seen. I was starting to understand why. I was an American in Europe and as many Americans, I felt as if I was in another world. I found it hard to compare the natural beauty of this country to anything I had seen or known before. We curved around bends going East and then South and began our approach to Trier. I tried to get a glimpse of the city through the people sitting on the left side of the train, but I couldn't. We arrived in Trier and got off of the train. We walked through the train station and exited on the other side of the platform.

Chapter 18

WALKING DOWN THE STAIRS into the city I had a feeling of déjà vu. Really more like déjà vu to the 100th power. The smells, sights, the air and the buildings were so familiar. Jenny was fumbling with her map trying to find the river. She said, "Where's the river. If I can find that I can find the city center." I turned to her and stunned myself by saying, "I know where it is." As difficult as this is to explain, it was as if I had an aerial view of the city. I instinctively knew how to get anywhere we needed to go in Trier. I knew this city like the back of my hand. It still shocks me to think about that revelation. I had never been there. How could I know this place? I wasn't the only one gap- jawed. I started to walk and they followed.

We got to Porta Negra, the ancient portal into the city of Trier. To me, the Porta Negra looked beige and light colored, as if it had just been built when actually it was thousands of years old and turning black with age. I looked down and then back up and the Porta Negra looked just as it is, old and ancient.

Walking through Porta Negra gave me chills. As we passed into the medieval part of Trier, which is the city center, I noticed the buildings had been freshly painted to reflect a more modern time, yet I could see how they looked long ago. This déjà vu continued throughout the morning. What was happening to me? Was I going crazy? During the rest of the morning, Jenny would ask me if I was alright every thirty minutes. I finally turned to face her feeling a little annoyed. I asked her why she kept asking me if I was alright. She said, "You look like you're in a daze." I replied, "I'm just concerned. Maybe, we should take a break and sit down and have a coffee." We found a little coffee shop in the city center and took a break.

I sat down with my sunglasses on and my eyes closed. I was trying to relax without anyone noticing. Under the shade of the canopy the spring breeze felt familiar. I took my sunglasses off when the waitress came with our coffee. I went to take a sip when I noticed in front of me a building. That's when it happened.

All time and space, the past and the present, melted into one moment that lasted for ten minutes. I felt as if I had been teleported into another time, but I was fully aware that I was still in the present. I could see myself sitting at the coffee house yet I wasn't really there. It was as if my body had split in two. In front of me was a young woman with blonde hair. It was shaped into a bun inside a type of netting. The netting connected to the headdress shaped like a donut roll. She was dressed in a beautiful sea blue renaissance gown, with diamonds sewn on. I tell myself, I know this girl and this place. I've dreamed it.

The girl continued walking towards the building and a tall thin man with a fur coat followed behind her. I followed them to see what would happen. They went to the top floor of the building, which was the fourth floor and the room is just the way I saw it in my dream. The columns were made of wood and the window was open.

The whole scenario played out exactly as it did in my dream. Just as I think the dream is about to be over, I see him down below walking through the street; the man I have been waiting for to take me away from this place. I felt so much love for him. But what was happening? Who were those men with him? I ran out of the room and down the stairs and out of the building towards him. I heard my own voice call his name, "Julian!" Then I ran towards him and wrapped my arms around his neck, but he didn't return my embrace. I look at him and I saw fear and sorrow and stains of tears on his face. One of the men pushed me back away from him and grabbed my hands and tied them in front of me. That is when I noticed Julian's hands were tied behind his back.

I scream, "NO!" in a language that is not English. "What are you doing, what is happening?" I turn and look for my regent in the crowd that surrounds me and Julian and the men holding us. I spot him and I yell out, "Tell them they are making a mistake! For God's sake tell them!" Then I notice the regent's familiar hateful smile and I understand what all of this means. What my regent has done to keep my (now his) wealth and to get rid of Julian and I. I stare at him as the pain of hurt, betrayal and anger fill my heart. Then he notices that the crowd has placed their attention on him. This makes him uncomfortable. I yell out with a hate I have never known before. "Your life will never have peace, only pain and sorrow will accompany you for the rest of your days." I see fear in his eyes and he turns and walks away. At that moment I hear someone say, "Silence her." I then hear a crack and feel a piercing pain from the top of my head that goes through my body like a lightning bolt. I look to Julian and hear him scream, "NO!" Julian tries to jump toward me as if to grab me, but those horrible, self-righteous men hold him back. Then everything fades away.

I wake up slowly. I try to adjust my sight but it is too dark. The smell of urine and feces are strong. I try to get up but I can't. My head aches and I lift my hand to touch my head. There is no hair. Where is my hair? I gently touch my head examining and trying to understand what has happened. I feel the large knot on my head and also the cuts from the blade that has shaved my hair off. I feel patches of hair and dried blood and I think I'm in shock. Can this really be happening? Fear sweeps in and I begin to cry. My thoughts go to Julian. Where is he? Is he alright?

I touch something on the ground. It's a dead rat and I scream. I try to jump up to get away but as I do, I'm jerked back from the ankle chain that is connected to the wall. I fall hard, landing on my back and that's when I notice that I'm not in my dress but in a thin gauzy gown. I try to catch my breath but I struggle to because I have just knocked the wind out of my body. I finally settle down and start to breathe with effort. I try to find my way in the dark back to the stone wall. I sit still and the realization comes that I will never leave this place, this cell. There is no one that will come and save me and the only person who can is in this horrible place with me.

I fall asleep only to be awakened to the sound of rattling keys and a door being unlocked. I slowly raise my head and I can barely see two guards with torches coming. I raise my hand to shield my eyes from the light that makes them burn. They unlock the ankle cuff and stand me up. I look to the tallest guard and ask him, "Am I free?"

He laughs and says, "No, witch!"

"I'm not a witch," I tell him as I raise my voice. "I'm a Jewish patron of this city."

The man responds, "A witch and a Jew, worse for you."

I'm stunned by his words. They push me towards the door and walk me down two flights of stairs. I go through the door and look in. I'm in a large chamber. There are implements of torture everywhere. My eyes widen with fear and I turn to run out of the room but they grab me and hold me back.

A deep voice comes out of nowhere and tells the guards to place me on the rack. I jerk and scream and fight to get away, but they have already tied me down. I see a man with a hood over his head and another with a book in his hand and he seems to be a priest. He is dressed in black and grossly fat. He gets close to me and scans my face for any marks. I can smell his foul breath and it makes me sick.

He says, "Let us begin. Do you admit to being a witch and consorting with the devil?"

"No!" I yelled. Then he looks to the man in the hood and nods a yes. I can hear the crank of the table. Then I feel the table start to pull my body.

I look to the priest and ask him, "Why are you doing this to me?" No answer.

Excruciating pain goes through my body and I began to scream.

Again he asks me the question, "Are you a witch?" I can't hear them because of the pain that I'm trying to bear. I begin to pray to God to stop all of this. If this is all a nightmare let me wake up. But it isn't a nightmare, this is all so real and I'm living it. Then I hear other questions and accusations of mating with the devil. Then I hear the priest say, "Get the pear."

Chapter 19

THE PAIN IS TOO much and I'm screaming at the top of my lungs. My breathing is labored. Then I see the guards and they began to open my mouth with an instrument. The priest continues his questions and I can hear popping and breaking of bones in my face. My body is pulled apart as limbs are pulled from their sockets and muscle and tendons are torn. I just want him to stop. Please God tell them to stop and that's when, from teary eyes, I look at the priest and nod my head yes to all his questions. Then I pass out.

I feel something rough on my face. A faint smell of grass mixed with urine as I slowly breathe in and out. I can't move. I try but pain passes through my body and almost makes me pass out again. I hear the door unlock and a dread comes over me. The same guards pull me up and I moan with pain. They get me up and turn me around. They take my dress off. I'm standing there naked and broken. One of the guards brings a metal bucket. Then I hear the tallest guard say in that strange language I understand, "She shat upon herself," then they both laugh. The tallest guard throws ice cold water on my back side and I jump because the cold causes more pain. Then they place a clean white linen shift on me.

They force me to walk up the stairs and in to a large room. My body, mind and soul are numb with pain, sorrow, confusion. I stand as best I can, but I feel as if I will pass out. Then I notice all the priest and bishops watching me.

I hear a door open and I raise my head and eyes towards the door. It is a man who has had his hair cut off and has been put to the rack like I have. Then I look again and tears began to fall and silently I sob. It's Julian. This once beautiful man was now gone. As he came closer to me I saw him staring at me in horror. His eyes wild with movement searching for someone that was not there. Not anymore. Tears ran down his cheeks. We stood by each other. He got close enough to touch my hand. Our heads hanging down toward the ground, we listen with what is left of our energy. We are being sentenced to death by fire.

Julian and I were escorted out of the building onto a cart with other people awaiting death. The cart began to move through the city and we are being taken somewhere far off into the woods. Julian holds my hand and I look at him as he says, "Be strong my beloved, I will always love you till the end of time itself. Don't let fear pass through your body, be strong, I'm near you." He is holding back tears of sadness.

I look around me and see women, children and men. They are all dressed like Julian and I. They all have their hair cut off and have been tortured. I notice one of the mothers pull out a vial and give some liquid to her child and then she passes the vial on to the other women to give to the children. I know what this is; it is dwale (belladonna) enough of it will put someone to sleep forever. The women do not want the children to feel the pain of fire upon their little bodies. I heard myself sobbing silently for them and for all of us. Why would men of God do this? The world was crazy and filled with greedy and arrogant men. But they think they are gods to judge us so harshly. Just as my regent, my own cousin, covets my property and will do anything to obtain it. These so called men of God want the same. They need to gain control of the world and get rid of those they saw as unfit for their paradise.

The cart stops and we are all marched out to our pyres. The children are already feeling the effects of the poison. Julian and I are placed next to each other, tied tightly to the post. I hear people crying. I hear curses spit out by others that are watching. Then I hear Julian say, "Look at me my love, look at me. Don't stop looking at me." My eyes lock on him and I never turn to look anywhere else. I hear the priest ask us if we want to admit our guilt to God. I ignore his words and so do the others. Then I hear and smell the crackling fire. It had begun. I hear terrible screams from others around us. Julian again says, "Keep looking at me" louder than before.

I see the smoke rising and it was obscuring my vision of Julian. Then I feel the pain of fire burning my feet. I want all this to end quickly. I want to die. I do not want to feel any pain or hear the cries of others. I yell out, "Please God take us all." I'm now breathing in the noxious smoke, great gulps of it and I felt dizzy and sick, then nothing. No cries. No Julian. Just darkness before me. I was finally at peace.

My soul returned to my body at full force. I was back to the present moment. Tears were running down my face and I saw Jenny looking at me with concern. "Are you alright?" she asked me with a slight quiver in her voice.

I wiped my face and took a deep breath. I was shaken and confused. I looked around me and saw Hans looking at me like I had antlers growing out of my head. I could see a plaque on the front of the building. "What is the name written on this building," I asked him. He said, "What?" Again, I repeated the question and pointed to the building in front of me. He placed his hands in a tent and said, "The Three Kings' House." My eyes widened and I said, "It was you!" Hans stared at me with confusion then contempt and I could see how uncomfortable he was becoming. He just walked away from us. I stared at his back as he walked away, my eyes two hot coals. I have never felt such loathing, such hate for any human being in my life as I did for Hans at that moment.

I turned and told Jenny and her husband, Pablo, that I needed to get to the hotel. Pablo went and got Hans and silently we walked back to the train station. The ride back was much the same as the ride to the site. Hans, again, was not sitting with us. He was further in front of us sitting in the seat facing me. He wouldn't stop looking at me. He was angry with me. I could feel the negative energy that he was projecting. But, I wasn't going to let him place fear in me so I stared right back at him. Again, this made him uncomfortable so he opened his book and placed it in front of him. Did he know what I was accusing him of? Did he understand what I meant?

Now, I understood why I disliked Hans when I first met him. How strange that I would come all this way to see a place I have never been to in this life and see the building that has been reoccurring in my dreams. But most of all, to meet the man that caused me and my lover so much pain and sorrow.

Could all of this be possible? It must be. Or maybe I'm crazy. All I know is that I had a horrible headache and just wanted to get some rest. The train ride seemed longer than usual. I was glad when we all entered the hotel.

Chapter 20

I MADE MY WAY TO my room. A good long drink sounded good to me and I usually don't drink. My room was fresh and cool. I closed the curtains and started taking every stitch of clothing off of me. I went to the bath and turned the faucets to warm water. Filling the tub, I used shampoo for bubble bath to have some type of floral aroma around me. I sank in to the tub taking deep breathes to relax.

The migraine I had would not let up. My mind was flooded with so many questions and no answers. I sat in the tub for about a half an hour then got out and dried myself off. I slipped my pajamas on and got under the covers in the dark room. The darkness put me back in that cell and I got up again and turned the light the bathroom light on, closing the door so that a thin stream of light came through. My head hit the pillow gently and I fell into a deep sleep.

I was awakened by a knocking and Jenny calling out to me asking if she could come in and check on me. I raised my head but it still ached. I slowly moved out of the bed and shuffled towards the door and opened it. The light from the hallway made my vision blurry and all I could see was Jenny's silhouette. "Oh God, you look bad sweetie," she said with concern. She came in and turned a lamp on. I went and crawled into bed. "Everyone is concerned about you. Have you taken anything for the headache?" I shook my head no. She opened her bag and pulled out some Advil and gave me four. "This is prescription strength. It should help." She went and got glass of water and gave me the pills. I downed them and drank all the water. "Thank you," I said.

"Hans went back home. He was upset about what you said. I don't know if he will continue with the research." I said nothing. "Why don't you tell me, if you can, what happened in Trier. It might help to talk about it." I looked at her and thought maybe she's right. I can't even understand what happened. I knew she would think me crazy and more than a little weird. I cleared my throat. "I don't know what your beliefs are, but mine are more towards the metaphysical. Do you believe in past lives?" I said this with apprehension. She smiled and said, "I'm a Buddhist, so yes, I do believe in past lives." I was so relieved. I went on to tell her exactly what happened and why I said that to Hans. Time went on and minutes and hours passed and I found myself sobbing with the recognition of loss of my beloved and betrayal of a family member. The suffering I felt for all those people who died with Julian and me. It was all so senseless, so cruel and heartless.

Jenny explained that I went through some type of portal. She said I needed to be there and that everything that happened up to this point in my life was bringing me here to this place for spiritual enlightenment. To be awakened from the material world and placed in a state of awareness about where I came from and what happened in the past. "You never wanted to forget," is what she told me. "Everything will become clearer soon. You will get your questions answered, just be patient." She left me to get some rest for the next day. Maybe I wasn't crazy. Jenny didn't think so.

We were invited, by Dr. Lansky's friend, to go to the Catholic Church for mass on Sunday to celebrate the Pentecost weekend. It was a special mass with opera and orchestra. I will never forget it; The Cathedral of Trier, inside the dom. *Agnus Dei, Mozart's Requiem.* It is one of the most beautiful arias I have ever heard and tears streamed down my face as I listened. Music is a language that transcends all linguistic barriers. The music, the events of the past few days and the realization that three hundred-sixty eight people died for their humble beliefs at the Trier Witch Trials, so long ago, made me feel overcome with emotion.

Chapter 21

SEVERAL DAYS INTO OUR little expedition, I woke up with another headache; however, not as intense as before. I showered and dressed and collected my backpack. I met everyone downstairs in the lobby. I noticed Hans was not with us, but Greg came on the early morning train. Nothing was said about Hans, though I could tell that Greg was worried and probably wondering what happened. I put my sunglasses on and we started another day of research.

Greg and I went to the Cathedral and Jenny and Pablo went to city hall for the records they needed to find. The Baroque cathedral in the city of Saarburg was magnificent. Light blue and pale white paint colored the walls of the aging church. Gold trim covered many of the surfaces and the Virgin Mary with Child was also covered in gold, her face the color of new snow. In the church there was a casket made entirely of clear glass. This was the casket of a saint, quite macabre, although not one recognized by the Catholic Church in the Canon of Saints. To the town of Saarburg he was a saint and was recognized for all that he had done for the people of this tiny town; whatever that may have been. I could not find anyone that knew what he had done to be a saint. I did some research on Saint Orana a beloved German Saint and realized that in some European countries, "saints" are not recognized by the Holy Roman Catholic Church; however, the diocese of Germany and some other countries in Europe recognize them as saints. This was the case with the saint in Saarburg.

As I stood there, looking at this collection of bones wrapped in fine satin, my mind took me back to the profound experience that occurred yesterday. A switch clicked. Now I understood. This man was not dead. The vessel he was born in was dead but not his soul. Even now with his bones lying there in the glass and gold leaf casket, he was still remembered for all he had done for this town and its people. So he would never be forgotten in either world. His soul would live on and renew again and so would the memory of the man he was in that time period. How extraordinary. Even when he is incarnated into another life, he could forget the man he was and all the history of that past life or maybe not.

Again my head ached and I felt drained. At times it seemed as if I had vertigo. Maybe I should go and see a doctor. I could not explain to the doctor what caused my headache in the first place. As I was pondering this, Greg asked me if I was alright. His question took me away from my thoughts. I answered, "Yes." I realized why he had asked me the question. I had stopped taking photos.

I slogged through the next two days with a considerable headache. But, on the third day something strange occurred. Whenever I would look at someone on the street, their features would change. They seemed to change into someone else as I was looking at them. I noticed the people I was focusing on were looking at me, too, in a peculiar manner. This didn't occur with everyone but it seemed like it. Now, I really thought something was wrong. I needed to talk with someone. I had to find out what made me see these people shape shift before my eyes. I was scared and alone with no one to guide me through this.

Days went by and no relief from this horror. I began to pray every night for God to take this away but I guess he wasn't listening.

I continued to see this shape shifting of people while they were walking in and out of cafes, coming off trains and just generally going about their business. I would see them and their faces would change to

Asians, Indians; and African - every ethnic culture would cross their faces. Their clothing would change to reflect different time periods. I was in a surreal zone. Would I ever wake from this nightmare?

Two weeks passed and we had been to several different cities and villages in south, west and East Germany. It had been decided that we would go to the South of France in two days. Even though I was in a perpetual nightmare, I was somewhat excited to be going to a place I had always dreamed of going.

We all had dinner, as usual, but it was announced that we would all be working together in the same cities. Hans, who had blessed us with his presence once again a week ago didn't care for this discussion. As I sat there looking at him. I could see that he was *the* regent in that past life. Have I been seeing past lives of the people that pass by me in the villages and cities? I turned around and looked at the friends with whom I was dining. They too would shape shift into other people from long ago. I finally got the nerve to talk with Jenny about what had been happening to me. She was surprised. She asked me to tell her what I saw with her and so I did and to my amazement I could feel the sorrow, happiness, anxiety and loneliness that had occurred in one of her past lives.

I explained that I saw her in a room all alone and bound by a long chain that connected to a stone wall. Her dress was filthy and her dark hair was greasy. The room was small and there was a bed pan next to her. Jenny asked me, "What happened to me?" I replied, "I think you were put there by your husband." Jenny was now more curious than before. "Go on" she said. I went on. "I can see the reason why you were placed in that room. It is a place where they take the mentally insane. Jenny's eyes widened. I continued. "I can see that you had been very happy once but tragedy occurred within your family. You were married and happy and your sickly father lived with you and your husband. I see a man, a stranger, walking to your cottage to ask for food. He raped you and murdered your father. This traumatic episode caused you to break from reality; it made you go insane. That's how you coped. After a while your husband couldn't handle you. You are afraid of the dark and you have night terrors of someone coming for you. You don't want to be left alone. You worry constantly. The guilt you feel is because you couldn't save your father and you are so angry at your husband for not being there. You still feel abandoned."

I stopped talking because I noticed Jenny crying. Why do I know this about her? I have said too much. "Jenny I'm sorry," I said. I had upset her. She looked up at me. "How do you know all this," she asked me between sobs. "There is no way you could have known that I was placed in a mental institution for the same problems of which you spoke." "I didn't know at all," I told her. "I wasn't talking about this life time. I saw this in a different time period." I told her I thought she was placed in an institution in England. She looked at me, shocked. "I thought you were talking about when I was younger... in this life," she said.

"No Jenny... I was talking about another life time." I repeated. Jenny got up and told me she had to go get ready for our trip to France. I could tell Jenny just wanted to leave. I shouldn't have said that to her and how in the world did I know all of that? I sat in silence for a while pondering all that I had said and what just had happened. I saw her life in my mind. But most of all I could feel that she had not learned from prior mistakes and it was taking a toll on her. What was going on with me? Why was I able to see her past lives? I was intrigued and ashamed at the same time. It brought up as much pain for me as it did for Jenny. I just wanted to make it up to her. I only hoped I could.

Chapter 22

I WAS EXHAUSTED AT THE end of a long day, but sleep did not come easily. I had mixed dreams that did not make sense and reoccurring dreams that did. I kept dreaming about a past life I had when I was very young; the one with the castle and my grandparents. I had other dreams like the mountain and the castle on top and running through the woods where I jumped to my death. Then I woke up, jerking the covers off of me. I was angry. This was driving me insane. During the day it was watching people shape shift and at night I couldn't sleep thinking about what all of this meant. If I didn't get help I would be going to a mental facility, just as Jenny had, and soon.

The next day, I awoke to an unseasonably cool May morning. The window was open and I grabbed my clothes, dressed and ran down to the lobby to check out.

Dr. Lansky walked up beside me. As I turned to look at him, I saw his eyes narrow and his forehead crease. "Are you alright?" he said, sounding somewhat alarmed.

"Yes." I said sounding annoyed.

"You're not getting sick are you?" Now, he sounded concerned.

"No... I just... had a sleepless night, that's all."

"Well we will all have two days to rest in the South of France," he replied.

"I think everyone needs a little vacation. You've all worked very hard for me and I want you to be able to relax for a couple of days. How does that sound to you?"

"That sounds great to me." I replied. I felt relieved he didn't continue to question me.

Dr. Lansky said, "Go and take your baggage to one of the vans. The driver will help you."

As I walked outside, I felt the cold crisp air hit my face. The temperature had dropped the night before and the temperature gauge at the register counter read 50 degrees. I looked at the vans. In the first van I could see Mrs. Lansky on the passenger side, along with three other researchers and Hans who was looking smug. I walked to the other van. The driver took my luggage and placed it in the back of the van. I got in and settled into the second row of seats in the van. Then I saw Jenny and Pablo coming my way. They both got in and Greg sat in the front seat. No one spoke during the entire ride to the airport.

We boarded the plane at Frankfurt Hahn airport and the silence among the group continued. The only sound came from the hum of the engines. I fell asleep an hour before we landed. Again I dreamt of past lives. I awoke with a start to the sound of the pilot telling us that we would be landing soon. Jenny was sitting by me and turned to me when she noticed I was awake.

"I thought about what you said and I spoke to Pablo about it," she said, speaking louder than the engine. "You're right that past life does coincide with this life. I guess I have a lot to work on. You came to me for help and I wasn't there for you. For that I'm sorry. But I want you to know that you have helped me understand more about myself and what I must do to let go. She touched my hand and squeezed it lightly." This was her way of letting me know everything was fine between us. I was relieved.

My headache was gone and even though strange situations happened that I still did not fully understand, I have found a new light within. I have enjoyed this adventure and I wouldn't change my experiences for anything. I know I will learn more in France. I know this because I can feel that something amazing is about to happen. Upon arrival at the Montpellier airport, I noticed military men with machine guns and dogs; very large German Shepherds. It was a little unsettling.

Chapter 23

A<small>FTER LANDING IN</small> M<small>ONTPELLIER</small>, France which is about six miles away from the Mediterranean Sea, we went through customs and out into the sunless, overcast day, I knew I had been to this place before. As I looked around, a vision of a woman on horseback riding through the valley appeared. She was wearing a dark red, thick velvet cloak with thick brown fur around the hood and down the cloak. She was accompanied by a man who was also on horseback. It was winter and fresh snow blanketed the ground on which the horses trod. The man looked like a monk but, for some reason, I knew he wasn't. He was an old friend of hers. She was past her prime child bearing years. I knew her very well. She was a healer traveling from village to village helping anyone that needed her expertise. Then the vision was gone. I smiled realizing that I had no reason to fear anything or any visions, dreams or even my past. This woman was me. At that moment I surrendered to the will. Whatever happens I will look at this as an experience. I would understand all of this soon. I just had to be patient.

Driving through the countryside and through the villages of Provence, I could feel my heart beating fast with excitement. Seeing the lavender fields against the backdrop of cottages, cypress trees, vineyards and hills gave me the feeling I was home; that I had come back from being gone for a very long time. The energy of the place was incredible. It literally gave me goose bumps, (confirmation). The universe was confirming what my soul already knew. I had lived in this part of France and up in the Pyrenees mountains.

I roamed and moved from village to village in a very distant past. I had felt the same way about Germany. I love that country and all its glory and rich landscapes and picturesque villages and castles. When we first arrived in Germany, I was apprehensive about being there due to past life experiences during World War II – but that's another time and another story. When we went to Munich, I was so uncomfortable being in that city. I was paranoid and scared to leave my room. The dislike I felt was so overwhelming that I had to leave the city of Munich with the other team the next day. I found out a few years later why I couldn't stand to be in there. There were beautiful memories of Germany, too. Like I said, that is another story.

As we reached the city of Carcassonne, which the people of that region called "la cite." you could see the huge fortified village with the castle of the viscounts within. It is located in the Languedoc-Roussillon region of Southern France. The first signs of settlement were the Celtics when they moved in to the region in 3500 B.C. Then later, Carcassonne was founded by the Visigoths in the 5th century but had been fortified by the Romans earlier. The city has seen many rulers but none can compare to the family of Trencavel; the viscounts of Albi and Nimes. The Trencavel family had tolerance of other religions in Carcassonne and cared and protected their people. The language spoken at the time was Occitan. Occitan is known also as **Lenga d'òc** (Occitan: French: *Langue d'oc*), is a Romantic language spoken in southern France.* Occitan descended from the spoken Latin language of the Roman Empire. Carcassonne became famous in its role in the Albigensian Crusades, when the city was a stronghold of Occitan Cathars. In August, 1209, the crusading army of Simon de Montfort forced its citizens to surrender. Raymond-Roger de Trencavel was imprisoned while negotiating his city's surrender and held in his own dungeon and allowed to die.

---

* **Sources:** Historic Fortified City of Carcassonne-Unesco, The Cathars and the Albigensian Crusade by Michael Costen, Regional Pronunciation-Occitan, Oxford Advanced Learner's Dictionary

The energy is ancient and mysterious in this part of France. It fills you with wonder, adventure and intrigue. The faith of so many lingers in the air here. It's almost palpable. The Languedoc region of France has seen war, death, birth, natural disaster, faith, hope and love within its culture. New beginnings and endings all wrapped up in thousands of years of history. Now, I know why so many people around the world love to visit Europe. With every breath, you take you can smell the richness of lavender, currant, pine, rose, and the entire flora that grow in this region. It is intoxicating.

We drove into the fortified city. The streets are narrow and curving through the stone covered ivy buildings of this small village. Cafes opened and the people enjoyed their moments of peace before the day began. We stopped in front of the Hotel de La Cite. I was mesmerized by the architecture of the building, taking me back in time to the medieval period. The gorgeous Hotel de La Cite sits in the heart of this medieval fortress.

Two van drivers dropped us off with our luggage. The vans had to be parked outside of the fortress. Only residents have the right to park their cars on the stone cobbled streets. Walking through the heavy wooden doors you actually felt as if you were royalty and the servants were waiting for you to arrive back home to the Chateau. Dr. Lansky wanted to treat us to a two night stay in the fortress. This would be our little vacation. We were honored and very pleased by his generous gesture. Rachel (one of the researchers) and I would be sharing a junior suite together.

We were taken up to our room. The door opened and we found ourselves face to face with the maid. She spoke to us in French and Rachel spoke back; very well I might add. Rachel informed me that she was making sure we had enough towels, coffee, tea, etc. in our room. I looked all around me. This is what it would be like to stay in a medieval castle hundreds of years ago, but with some small amenities and advances. The stone fireplace was lit as the room was very cold.

I went toward the French doors that opened onto the balcony. The clouds were a dark grey filled with rain. Thunder, lightning, wind and rain would put me back in my element; inclement weather. Nothing and no one could change the way I felt at that moment. I was filled with memories and a feeling of home. It was such a comforting feeling. I felt as if I were home, really home. I found myself wishing my two boys were there. Now, that would make it all complete.

The next few days brought more visions/dreams as I walked around the fortress; visions of me as a young girl going in the Basilica of Saint-Nazaire, a Knight Templar walking by The Chateau, Comtal, a little girl and boy running towards the river Aude but in different time periods. I was fascinated and stunned at how much I knew this city inside and out. Just like Trier. Was this my imagination or was I really here in those time periods? Was it the moment of being somewhere else where no one knew you? I just didn't know any of the answers. We would be leaving the next day for Montségur and that, too, sounded familiar. My heart ached. I did not want to leave this place. I was dreading the ride to the places we needed to go. I felt safe here and at peace.

The weather changed and even though it was getting close to summer, the temperature would cool down at night. I was walking the streets alone when a man came up to me speaking in French. His blue eyes almost seemed crystalline. He was a tall built man maybe in his early fifties, with dark brown hair graying on the sides. I explained I only knew a little French. "Oh American," he said in a rough accent. "Would you like for me to tell your fortune?" I thought about it, and then agreed to the fortune telling.

He directed me toward a small table where the shop owner was sitting. The shop owner got up and a woman came out wiping her hands on her apron. She asked me if I wanted coffee. I said "Yes please," in French. I looked around. The hotel was not far away and there were people walking the streets. A group of British people, I could hear their accent, passed by and sat four tables down from us.

The French fortune teller began shuffling a deck of cards I had never seen before. They were beautiful, old looking and covered in gold trim. He had me pick thirteen cards from the deck and he placed them in a circle as I gave them to him. In his broken English, although he did speak English well regardless of his thick French accent, he began to read the signs the cards gave to him. "You are following a path that you made for yourself long ago." "What Path?" I asked. He continued. "Let us say you made a contract before you were born." A contract with whom? I thought. My forehead creased as I looked at him and I was a little afraid of what he might say. He went on. "You have never wanted to forget who you are. I mean your soul, the true essence of *you*. There have been past lives when you had no connection to your soul and you were lost in this material world. The shell that houses your soul took over and you made terrible mistakes that cost you much in those life times. You lost your way and now you want to stay on your path." "Do you mean like the ego of a person?" I asked. "Yes exactly. You have already had many changes, profound changes. There will be many changes to come. Soon I think. Yes soon." "I don't like changes, it causes me so much pain," I said to him. He smiled at me sympathetically, "Change is good even if it is bad. Change creates life lessons which we all have to learn from. What I see here is that you have been opened up to your higher self to the god/goddess within you, to your gifts and this is not a coincidence. This is what you wanted to happen. You need to connect to your soul out of unconditional love for yourself and others. You have been insane most of your life and now you are finally reaching sanity because you are connecting to the one thing that is important **Your Soul**. You recognize it now. What wonderful sight you have. Your life path will lead you to others who will need to find their soul and come out of the insane world they live in. This is your fate, your destiny. Everything that has happened to bring you to this point, bad or good, was orchestrated by you before you were even in the womb of your mother. So be fearless. Walk in your lighted path. Love your true being and take care of the shell. Walk in unconditional love; do not be afraid to give and never expect to receive. Because giving is what lights up your soul and loving nourishes the soul." I stayed silent for a moment.

Then I looked at him. "Thank you very much for the reading. You have answered a lot of questions I could not answer for myself." "You would have found the answers you are seeking. I don't doubt that," he said smiling again. "Thank you. What do I owe you?" Again he smiled and said, "Nothing." As he said this he placed his hands together and slid them across each other like wiping a slate clean." I have to give you some type of exchange." He shook his head no. "I was told that you needed answers because you were ready to see the light of yourself. "Who told you that?" I said. He smiled that permanent smile etched on his face and leaned in closer to me and looking straight into my eyes, he said to me, "The Master sent me to you."

I sat back a little, still looking at him dumb-founded. Chills ran up and down my spine as he said that to me. Then I knew who he was talking about, God. I smiled back and thanked him again. "Oh, there is one more thing you must know. They have told me that one day in the future you will find your true partner, your twin, the person that equals you in energy and personality. He will be coming your way when you are ready. Do not linger on this thought. Let this happen naturally. There are so many things you must do for yourself first and for others before you meet."

I thanked him again and turned and walked away towards the hotel. I stopped because I really needed to give him compensation for his time. When I turned around thinking that I would see him sitting, waiting to read for someone, there was no one there. I only walked ten or fifteen yards. I could still see the café and the chairs and tables. But the strange thing was the café was closed and the British people were gone. He was gone.

I had only walked for about fifteen seconds. I walked back and looked up and down the street and inside the café. I saw no one. I stood there for a while trying to comprehend what had just happened. Then I noticed a shiny object under the table. I bent down to retrieve it. It was a medal of some kind. When I held it up to the light post I saw it was a medal of Archangel Michael. I looked around again, and then I began to walk back to the hotel. Could I have had an encounter with an angel, an archangel? I looked back at the café one more time. Everything happens for a reason. No coincidences only synchronicities. I shook my head in disbelief and began to laugh quietly at all the miracles that were being sent my way. "Ask, and it will be given to you; seek, and you will find; knock, and it will be opened to you."* I was receiving loud and clear now. I had total clarity thanks to God and to divine guidance which help me stay on my path.

*King James Bible, Matthew 7:7

Chapter 24

WE WERE ON OUR way to Montségur. I could feel that something, although I wasn't sure quite what, would become evident to me in this place, so I tried to make as myself ready to receive any information given.

You are never ready when Spirit takes you to a place that you have already known in a different time. The familiar mountain was visible from the road. As we drove closer I could see the ruins of the castle top. This place had so much significance to me. When we drove up and got out of the van, I looked up to see the place I had dreamt about for so long; the place where I jumped to my death. Montségur was the last stronghold of the heretics the Catholic Church called Cathars. The Pog (the foot of the mountain) is approximately where 224 Cathars were burned on a pyre.* The mountain sits in the region of the Midi-Pyrenees. In the middle ages, the Montségur region was ruled by the Counts of Toulouse, the Viscounts of Carcassonne and finally the Counts of Foix. In 1243–44, the Cathars were besieged at Montségur by 10,000 troops at the end of the Albigensian Crusade.* Good men, women and children surrendered and walked into a funeral pyre to be burned to death for their beliefs.

* **Sources:** Russianbooks.org, hubpages.com, Cathar.info, The Albigensian Crusade by Jonathan Sumption

A deep sadness came over me and I knew I had to reach the top to find more answers. Getting there was difficult because the climb was steep and rocky. As we reached the top I could see the villages that surrounded Montségur. The Pyrenees Mountains were blue-green in color like the Caribbean Sea. As beautiful as the Caribbean is, there are grey days and standing on Montségur was a grey day filled with memories I would like to forget but, I can't. I was never *meant* to forget. I was destined to remember, always and in all times. Unlike my first experience in Montségur, all was quiet. No burnings, no yelling, no sound - only silence. The energy here was so sad, so depressing. The castle ruins were not the same ones I saw in my dream, but another that had been built later. I walked to the area that I knew. Now, I knew why I was afraid of heights. I tried to look down, but vertigo and nausea hit me and I kept looking straight ahead.

I walked away and sat down on the ground, taking deep breaths in and out. Tears ran down my face as if a faucet had been opened. I needed to release these feelings and leave them in Montségur. I now understood why I took my life there. Traditional religion states that if you take your own life, the unforgivable sin, you will go to hell. I took my own life in saving my spirit from assault, so that I would not carry that feeling into the next life time. I understood the consequences of this action being a Cathar at the time. The Cathars understood past lives and believed in them, too. They probably understood more than we do now. But let me just say this: I'm not condoning suicide. Life is precious and we are given many chances to make it right. We create our own hell and we can create our own heaven, too.

How many times must we repeat the gross injustices that riddle history? When will we learn? As we walk in this life we are bound to each other. We will repeat the lives we have lived over and over again until we learn that our ego cannot be the master of our lives. We must, as spiritual beings, connect to our world and each other. We must be as one; one collective mind. Without this, there will be no peace and no harmony. It is possible and imperative that we be as one with each other in unconditional love, working with each other and not against.

I sat there, rejoicing in the wonderment of the world, universe and life itself. Every color was brighter and fresh new eyes watched the sun set with new friends on this mountain of faith… Montségur.

Chapter 25

THE LAST LEG OF our trip was a visit to Puivert, France. This was unexpected. We were to research the castle there. I had done my own research regarding my grandparents during the time they lived in Puivert and I very much wanted to see this place. Synchronicity had been occurring on this trip; miracles and magic happened at every turn. Now, I would see the place I use to live; a village that I had no earthly idea existed until I dreamed about it in this life time.

We drove into the village late in the evening. I couldn't really see what the village looked like as the sun was only a sliver of light in the sky. We stayed in a house, in a nearby town, that was loaned to us by a friend of Greg's. As we passed through the village, against the back drop of the hills, I could see the castle or at least what was left of it. But, it did not seem to be like the castle I saw in my dream. The front part of the castle seemed the same and the other sections were in ruins. I would see more in the morning.

I couldn't really sleep more than a nod here and there and when I awoke, I was excited. Would I be given the chance to see where my grandparents lived in that life? We all met in the morning and sat down for breakfast. We were given our itineraries and I realized we had been separated by groups. The first group would consist of Dr. Lansky and his wife with three others going to Puivert. The next team would be me, Jenny, Pablo, and Greg heading to Foix. I was so disappointed. We came all this way but for what. There was nothing I could do. I had to go to Foix.

Sometimes we want to do other things or to go to other places even be with other people, then the universe steps in and gently nudges you in a different direction. Everything in your life happens for a reason. I know this now even though at the time I did not. Foix is a beautiful medieval village. The Castle Foix sits atop of great hill. Apparently, the Romans built a fort where the Castle Foix is now.

As we started out, I noticed a thick fog which surrounded the entire village. Spooky as it was at first, the village Foix took on a mysterious and mystical quality. I went with the others to a building where historical records were kept. I was appointed the task of looking up religious records dating back thousands of years. Dr. Lansky wanted to get a firm idea of the religious culture of the area and how it changed or stayed the same through the years. Research took my mind off the fact that I wouldn't be seeing Puivert.

The hours passed and I came across papers that documented the time period of the Albigensian Crusade. At the time, the counts of the village of Foix accepted Cathars and protected them against persecution; even though Simon de Montfort besieged the castle. The people of Foix resisted the assault of the Crusaders. Not until much later did the castle fall into enemy hands. As I continued to read the documents, I realized that there was a possibility that my grandparents had been saved. Maybe they had come here for protection. I could only hope. That didn't change the feeling of guilt that I dealt with in this life time. I don't think I will ever know, at least not while I'm here in this dimension.

I began to realize that there were good and decent counts, kings and queens that truly cared for their people. But most of all, the Cathars showed us that actions speak so much louder than words. For two to three hundred years their religion flourished. They were true to their faith and belief's. We are all precious beings in the eyes of God. Why, then, do we live our lives separate from one another through religion, race, even our life styles and status. We even separate ourselves from our souls. We are all connected. We are one. Forever.

We went back to Puivert for dinner. I didn't know when I would ever return to Puivert. We planned to leave the next day and return to Germany and soon after, home. I just wanted a chance to look around this village. Then I thought if it is meant to be it will happen.

Well, it happened. One of the vans broke down and we had to stay in Puivert for the day while the van was being repaired. God heard my plea and I was so thankful. Jenny, Pablo and I went walking through the village. Some of the sites seemed familiar but some did not. We climbed up a hill that I remembered from my dream. I was scanning around looking for the area where my grandparents lived in that time. I didn't dare tell Jenny or Pablo what I was doing. I wanted this to be my own secret. I figured out where the house had once stood and we walked down into the city.

Walking among the houses I came upon one that looked familiar but I wasn't sure. An old gentleman came out of the house smoking a pipe. He looked at us. Then he smiled and said hello in English. We were surprised. We thought he was French. We walked over and I began to ask questions about the houses in this part of town. He told us that some of the old houses had been taken down from the medieval period. I described my grandparent's house to him as I recalled it from my dream. I asked him if he had ever seen a house in that area that fit the description. He thought for a moment then said, "When I was a little boy, my family owned a house here. We lived in England; however, my mother loved this part of the world. At one time it was her family home. My parents couldn't take care of it so they sold the old house. But from what you describe, that sounds like the house that used to be right here." He pointed to the house he and his wife lived in currently. The owners had torn down a good portion of the old structure and modernized it. He told us to wait for a moment and he went inside for a while. The old man came out and had some pictures in his hand. "Here, this is my mother and father," he said. I looked at the pictures. Then, I noticed the house that was behind them in the photo. It was the same one as in my dream. This was the house my grandparents lived in so long ago. I was shocked.

I really didn't know what to expect but I was surprised. I wanted to cry with happiness. I wasn't crazy. The dreams and visions that I have had since the age of five are real places that existed in that era, and parts of them exist to this day. The only thing I could utter, was "How miraculous." To know that your soul is truly immortal that you never die, just the body you inhabit passes. I thanked the man for his time and kindness. I looked once more at the picture. I had found what I was looking for. I was a changed woman; forever changed by an old photograph.

My time in Europe ended. It was time to go home, back to America. My trip to Europe was only six weeks, yet it seemed a lifetime. My time there was not without reason. I would find out more when I got back home, but for now life was brighter. I saw, with clarity that I had never possessed before my trip to Europe. I knew what my life purpose was. As I got on the plane, I sat by a man dressed in a military uniform and we began to talk.

He told me of his time in Germany and other countries to which he went. He said the one thing that bothered him was that some of European countries seemed so familiar to him, as if he had lived there before. What surprised him was that he knew every detail of the buildings and surroundings and even the names of roads in the villages he went to. "There is no way that I could have known this. I've never lived here before and history is not my forte," he said. He told me he was a devout Christian but he wondered if we really did have past lives like the Buddhists believe. I looked at him and smiled. "Yes," I said, "We have lived before many, many times. I know in my soul this is true."

I had no fear of flying as I looked out the window and saw Germany below. I was a happy woman with a new outlook and a new spiritual agenda.

Chapter 26

I RETURNED HOME TO FAMILY and friends; elated to see my boys. I had to admit that I was home sick for Germany and France. I had to get adjusted to my normal routine. I found a job and slowly came back to the life I have in America.

Two months went by quickly and I realized I was going down the wrong road again. I needed to stay focused on what my path was now. Balancing the material world and spiritual world was hard at times. Working on my ego was even harder. Looking at the person that you have become due to programs in this life and past karma was difficult. But, I was determined not to make the same mistakes. I did not want to separate my soul from my human self. I wanted them to be one and the same and I knew that this could be.

We are spiritual beings going through a human experience on this blue planet. I chose this life and I needed to know what I needed to learn. How could I go out there and help others if I couldn't help myself? How could I really love someone if I did not love myself? How could I heal someone else if I am not healed from past and current pain, fear and phobia? The bottom line is: You can't. My energy had shifted while I was in Europe. When I returned home, my boys said I was a happier person and I was.

I have remained at peace with myself and it's a work in progress. It's a struggle for all of us and I believe we have to continue to work on ourselves until the day we leave the physical world to travel into another spiritual realm.

I wanted to know more about my experiences in Germany and France. I did research on the history of those countries. Trier was first on my list. Since I had such a profound experience there I wanted to know what had happened in that time period. The period was around 1580-1600. I just knew that this was the right time period. As I was researching, I found out that the Catholic Church at the time decided to eliminate witches in Germany and it wasn't just witches. It was anyone who didn't believe as they espoused. So, that meant Jews and Protestants, nobility, government and administration were on the top of the Catholic Church's hit list. Johann Von Schoenberg was the fanatical leader of the non-conformity trials and he was responsible for the deaths of hundreds in Trier and around the diocese.

My experience was that my cousin, the regent, was intent on stealing my money, property and anything else he could get his hands on. If I were to marry, all of my worldly goods would have gone to my husband as a dowry. This is what was happening at that time; families going against each other in the name of money, power and greed. I died because I was naïve and young. The man who loved me died because he was about to marry me and was innocent. He unknowingly came at a time when I was about to be arrested for being a Jew and accused of witchcraft. Hans, part of our research team, was the man who sent Julian and I to our deaths. Even now, when I think about it, I'm still bewildered that a man that I never knew in this life would be working with me in Europe and was responsible for my death in another life time. I hated him for a good long time.

This hate kept me in a dark place. So, I forgave him for what he had done then and forgave myself for the guilt and the hate that I had for Hans in that past life. Suddenly, it was like a cloud lifted off of me and I was free. I could breathe. My heart was lighter and I was truly free from the bounds I had with Hans in that life. Closing the door on a past lives which didn't serve me at present, gave me the opportunity to bring a part of my soul energy back.

Now, I wonder why I had such a profound experience like I did in Trier. What happened? Did I teleport to that time? Was I there in Trier in the present or the past? I recently read a book by Pablo Coehlo called *"Aleph."* This book answered many of my questions. It's when time and space; past, present and future - stand still in one moment. This is the time when the door opens and you step in not leaving the present but bringing the moment of the past to the present. It's like a vortex: Sacred doors, openings, portals. Maybe, there was a vortex or portal in Trier and it took me to that place in the past. Or maybe, I was the portal, and I needed to actually be there to connect to the energy at that point with Hans. It made it easier to go through the veil with the two of us standing close together. This had to happen to enable me to see the truth.

Then there were the severe headaches after the experience of moving into the portal. I did my research on this, too. When someone has a near death experience, they come away, many times, with psychic abilities they did not possess before. They can communicate with the dead. Sometimes, they have another type of psychic ability, possibly repressed.

I kept my psychic ability blocked, out of fear of the implications it would have on my life. Psychic abilities can come after a person sustains a significant head injury. My experiences in Europe had awakened my senses. I realized that I had been born with the ability to see my own past lives and the past lives of others. Now, all the pieces of my puzzle were starting to fit. Slowly, I was using the gifts I had received to help others.

Every experience I had, from the time I was born until the time I actually saw my visions/dreams become a reality, and was guided by a divine hand. It was all meant to be. All the lessons I have learned have made me the person I am today. Lepkana was right. I made a contract to never forget who I really am. To always remember my soul.

Your soul is the library of your life; the memories of all that you have done and will do. We can change for the better if we really want to. We can raise our vibration in this world. We can lift the veil and see the true beauty in all people. Jesus said, "The Kingdom of God is within you."* This is true. We just have to be willing to find that kingdom. The kingdom is compassion, love, forgiveness and understanding of ourselves and of others who walk into our lives and those who we pass on the streets.

We are bound to others in different life times. We have to make amends or we will continue this cycle with every incarnation.

King James Bible, Luke 17:21

Chapter 27

I CHOSE THE LIFE I'm presently in. We all choose the life in which we reincarnate. I chose this life because of unresolved issues from past lives; to finish the Karmic cycle. To follow my path and to never forget who I really am now and who I was. I came back to connect to my own soul and help others in the process of finding their soul. Once we do this, we are one with the Divine, the universe and with one another. But, getting there can be difficult. Learning from our mistakes takes us to a higher level of awareness and closer to enlightenment. Forgiving ourselves is sometimes the most difficult thing to do. We seem to have the ability to forgive others with much more ease than we forgive ourselves, and it's difficult, at times, to forgive others. Love vibrates at an extremely high level, just as hate vibrates at an even stronger level. Which would you choose?

If there is one thing and one thing only that I hope to convey by writing this book, it is this: It is time we all wake up and come back to the spiritual beings we truly are. Our soul is immortal. I know that I must renew my soul with an energy that keeps me blissful even when everything is crashing down around me. Problems are temporary. Solutions can be permanent. I'm not afraid to walk my path of light. I am light. I am a part of God.

I see the world around me and what a negative state, we, as humans, are in. The world is unbalanced. But, I do know that there are individuals out there that truly care about the world, and all the people on this precious planet. We are unique individuals. Individuals that can come together as one if we truly try; we are all connected. We can make our heaven here and we can also make our own hell.

Living within the ego is not within our nature. We are spirit beings. I'm grateful for the experiences I have had and will continue to have. I understand that we all have free will. We have the will and ability to be positive more than negative. We are human and we live in a world that has to have balance. So, we must have balance within us and without us. We can look to the examples we have in the Ascended Masters. These individuals lived on this planet just like us. They made mistakes but learned, and in the process, raised their vibration to a higher awareness, to a higher spiritual level while still living on this planet.

Ascended Masters have shown us how to connect with our spiritual light within. How we, too, can be one within ourselves. I'm sure that they all had many past lives in order to get it right the last time. My guides, masters, teachers and loved ones have been guiding me through this life, nudging me here and there when I veer from my course. I listen and look for the signs. I will always have faith and believe in the fact that I will be guided to the place I need to be for the higher good of All. And, I include myself in the equation.

Unconditional love will open my heart connecting heart and soul. It *is* possible to use our energy with our eyes, mind and heart open. We will continue on our paths until the end of time as we know it and so much farther beyond that.

www.ingramcontent.com/pod-product-compliance
Lightning Source LLC
Chambersburg PA
CBHW051440280526
45785CB00003B/1359